When
Trouble
Comes

Contributors:

NORMAN L. BOWMAN   RAY COOLEY

FRANK GRAYUM   JAMES W. HATLEY

REUBEN HERRING   JOHN ISHEE

WALTER C. JACKSON   ALBERT MEIBURG

JEAN POTTS   JAMES M. ROBINSON

MICHAEL L. SPEER

When Trouble Comes

compiled by
John Ishee

Broadman Press
Nashville, Tennessee

The opinions of the persons speaking in this book are their own and do not necessarily reflect absolute coincidence with the views of the publisher

Library of Congress Catalog Card Number: 75–113211
Dewey Decimal Classification Number: 242.4
Printed in the United States of America
21.5Jy70KSP

Lingering in my memory is an experience that occurred while I was a student at Southern Baptist Theological Seminary in Louisville, Kentucky. In a course in pastoral care, Wayne E. Oates spoke of how tragic experiences often result in the development of positive attributes in one's character. One student, perhaps stung by the splendor of philosophical speculation, commented, "If what you say is true, it seems logical that people should seek tragedy in order to attain character." There was a long pause—the class waited. Then Dr. Oates replied, "When you have worked with people for awhile you will discover that trouble has a way of finding you. No one escapes it. If you live long enough, you will encounter it."

Perhaps the poet had this in mind when he wrote, "Don't you trouble trouble till trouble troubles you. Don't you look for trouble; let trouble look for you."

"Nobody Knows the Trouble I've Seen" is the title of a spiritual song. Perhaps its lasting popularity is due to the fact that it speaks of man's experience. Something within man's soul cries, "That's right."

Such experiences, however, equip us to be helpers to fellow pilgrims who experience trouble. This was the experience of our Lord Jesus who "being found in fashion as a man, he humbled himself, and became obedient unto death, even the death of the cross" (Phil. 2:8).

The case studies in this book cover a spectrum of problems

that cause uneasiness in the minds and souls of people. They
are not unlike experiences encountered by people we meet
in life. Moreover, they are not unlike experiences that we
inevitably encounter in life. The Christian who is concerned
with ministering to people must also concern himself with
learning how to help. He must learn how to help in order that
his efforts may produce fruit. He must know what to do, rather
than simply doing something.

Most books with titles similar to this one deal primarily
with sickness and death. Obviously, there are enumerable
problems that plague individuals in addition to these two.
This book recognizes that people in the drama of life encounter problems. Often these problems drain them of their
creative energies. It is the task of the Christian to help others
to "Bear ye one another's burdens, and so fulfil the law of
Christ" (Gal. 6:2).

The format of this book is simple. I asked eight persons
to write case studies out of their experience. Then I asked
a pastor and a hospital chaplain to write analyses of these
case studies from the point of view of how to help the individuals involved. Finally, I ventured to write my own analysis of each case study. The analyses of the case studies do not
seek to give the final answer. Actually, there are very few
final answers in helping people. This is true because there are
always three major variables in any situation. The first variable is the person in trouble. The second variable is the
person who is offering help. And, the third variable is the
situation in which the help is given. To change any one of
these three variables is likely to produce an entirely different
situation. Therefore, each of the analysts made suggestions
based upon the specific case study. Finally, the question is
asked, "How would you help this individual?" You are en-

couraged to think for yourself. In so doing, you should gain insight and skills that will help you to better minister to persons in trouble.

The final pages of this book contain suggested activities for use in groups. The book is coordinated with a record album by the same title. The book and the record album along with the training activities can form the basis for group study over a period of four to eight weeks. The exchange of opinions and information within a group can add new dimensions to the study.

I am indebted to all the writers for their very excellent cooperation in producing this book. Miss Barbara Lowry and Mrs. Linda Dunnavant were of immeasurable assistance in editing the manuscript for publication. Finally, a debt of gratitude is owed to Bill Cannon of Broadman Books for his receptivity to the idea and his cooperation during the production process.

JOHN ISHEE

CONTENTS

When
Trouble
Comes

"What's Happened to Our Marriage?"

Albert Meiburg

I met Brad and Julie just over a year ago. They were a young couple that lived in the community for three years. My first contact with them came when a member of our church suggested that I visit them. They joined our church, but in recent months I had not seen much of them.

About two weeks ago Julie had called me and asked if I could come to see her. Sensing that she was upset, I offered to come at once, but she preferred that I visit her the following evening when Brad would be at work. During our conference, she told me that Brad refused to give her any money for her own use and even restricted her to a set amount for groceries every week. Several times she had been embarrassed when she reached the cash register in the supermarket and found that because of insufficient cash she would have to return some items to the shelf. She said bitterly that in spite of Brad's concern over her spending, he always found it possible to buy whatever he wanted for himself.

After some discussion, I suggested that perhaps it would be helpful if I sat down with both Brad and Julie so that we could look at this matter together. Within several days I spoke to Brad, told him of my visit with Julie, and arranged to see them both on Brad's next free evening.

Brad met me at the door, shook my hand warmly, and took my coat. We engaged in small talk until Julie came back from putting their oldest child to bed. When we were all seated comfortably, I decided to get down to the business at hand.

"Well," I began, "as I told you at the office the other day, Brad, I chatted with Julie a few days ago and she seemed pretty upset. So it seemed to me a good idea for us to sit down and look at the situation together."

Brad said nothing, but looked at Julie, who lit up a cigarette.

I continued.

"I realize you might consider my interest as trespassing. But as a minister, invited to share a problem which really involves the two of you, I felt that this was really the only way to go about it."

Brad smiled at Julie, chuckled, and said, "I'm glad you came, but this isn't anything new. Julie has been complaining about money for the three years that we've been married and living here. She just doesn't have any idea about handling money."

Julie sat silently, simply looking at Brad.

"She's probably told you that I keep her to a tight budget," he continued, "and that I buy TV's, cars, and watches for myself. That's true, but those are the only things we own in this house. Not a stick of furniture belongs to us, and we have to save so that I can go to the university in the fall. She simply has no idea how tight things will be for us the next four years while I'm in school. We need every cent we can scrape together. We have to have a car and the television is the only piece of furniture we own."

Julie was very casual but direct in her reply. "And look where the car is. Up on blocks in the carport. You ride to work in the car pool but I can't drive anywhere until I go and pay for the insurance!

"And I'm pretty good when it comes to spending. I make all the clothes for the kids, as well as myself."

After a pause, Brad responded. "Well, I have to admit that you're pretty good that way. But if I didn't keep a tight rein on your allowance, you'd spend a lot more."

"I don't think so," Julie argued. "I might spend more on food. Brad, you don't have any idea how much groceries are these days. Milk is almost forty cents a quart and we use a lot. Timmie won't drink that powdered stuff even when I mix it half and half with whole milk. And besides, you always drink milk every meal. You'd have a fit if we switched over to powdered. But kids need lots of milk and eggs and fruits and vegetables. And when I run over on the grocery, you get mad!

"And another thing," she continued, "do you know that I never go to anybody else's house for coffee? On Tuesday, Helen drives out here and on Thursday, Alice calls in the afternoon. The only time I see anybody else is when I take your daughter to the swimming pool a couple of afternoons a week. That's not much of a visit."

There was a long pause. I broke the silence.

"Folks, there's quite a bit in what you've both been saying, but I'm a little confused. Brad, you say this is nothing new— arguing over money. But have the two of you ever tried to do anything about it? Every couple has to come to grips with the money question. Some try to agree together on a budget. Some have joint bank accounts. Have you ever tried anything like that?"

"Sure," said Brad. "I opened up a savings account for Julie and gave her some money."

"Fifty dollars!" exclaimed Julie. "And out of that I had to

buy our Christmas presents—the ones I couldn't make. I had enough to buy myself a dress and a pair of shoes. One dress for a whole year! That was your present to me! I have exactly $3.56 left!"

"Brad," I asked, "do you give Julie anything for personal items?"

"No, he doesn't," asserted Julie. "Pastor, I hardly ever get out to spend things in that way. If I chat with my friends, it's over here."

"I see," I said. "But both of you should have something to spend for incidentals and recreation."

"We don't do those things," Julie declared. "Brad works every bit of overtime he can. He draws up the shifts at work and always makes sure that he has Monday, Wednesday, and Friday nights off for weight training at the gym. Thursday and Tuesday nights he takes that bookkeeping course at the school. Some weekends, especially now that he's decided to go to the university, he works both days—sixteen hours a day."

There was a pause. I offered some feedback. "You know, as I listen to both of you, I'm getting the impression that you don't have a money problem as such. The problem is more basic, Brad. For some reason, whether it's money or not, you're not getting through to each other."

"I don't know," he demurred. "The only time Julie gets like this is when we get off on this 'I need some money' kick."

Julie, however, knew what I was trying to say. "Maybe he has a point, Brad. You know yourself that you're never home. There are days on end when the children never see you. You leave at 8:00 at night. Timmie isn't up when you leave and she's usually asleep when you come home. . . ."

She continued, "And you hardly pay any attention to me, unless I do something wrong. You just come home, demand your supper, and sit in there watching that dumb television!" I could see that her last remark got through to Brad.

"Okay," he said, raising his voice. "But if you worked sixteen hours a day and sometimes more, you wouldn't feel like talking when you got home either!"

"But Brad, we never talk. We argue. And you never play with the kids. And Timmie's at the point where I'm having a hard time taking care of her. She needs a father."

I sat back to see what was going to happen as a result of this encounter. There was a prolonged silence. I asked, "What seems to be happening to your marriage?" Again silence.

Brad chuckled as if suddenly thinking of something amusing. "I don't think there's anything wrong with our marriage. It's just Julie on her old kick. Everything, or just about everything, that's been said here tonight has been said before."

"I don't think so, Brad," Julie disagreed. "Look, do you think I would go to the trouble of calling Arnold if there wasn't something wrong with our marriage? You know very well it's been like this since we've been married. You insisted on getting married and coming right up North. You've always been used to having things your own way. If you didn't, you'd just go to your mother and she would take care of you. It doesn't seem to matter that she and I don't get along. And that's another thing—I have a pretty good idea when we go back South this fall, you'll just go and set up house with them. But I won't take that. You'll just tell me that if I don't go, I can just live with Mom. And on what? You wouldn't give me one red cent!

"Why don't you think about me once in a while?" Julie pleaded. "I cook for you, I raise your children, I keep this place clean, and I've fixed it up pretty comfortably by sewing slipcovers, curtains, and stuff like that. And you hardly ever speak to me! You're hardly ever at home. Yet you expect me to be happy without even going out once in a while." Tears were beginning to come to Julie's eyes.

"Do you know that we've only gone bowling once in the last couple of years! And all you did was sit there. You never talked to anybody. And when I was talking to Mike and Helen, you got mad when we got home and accused me of 'having a pretty good time with Mike tonight.'"

The flood gates were open and Julie's anger was pouring out.

"Brad, that kind of marriage where a wife is a slave is over! A husband and a wife have to do things together. Kids deserve a father who plays with them."

She turned to me.

"Arnold, Brad has always been possessive. Why when Timmie was born, he even threatened to hit the doctor because he wouldn't allow him in the delivery room! They finally had to usher him out of the hospital. He made a terrible scene! He makes accusations over even the most casual conversation!"

She shifted her attention back to Brad.

"Brad, there is something wrong with our marriage. I try to do what a wife and mother should. But I never get any thanks from you. The only time when you pay any attention to me is when you want a little sex. But I want our life together to be more than that. That's why I called Arnold over the other day —it's because I love you and the children, but I just can't go on like this!"

Brad just sat there for a while and said nothing. Julie kept looking at him. I kept hoping Brad would give some response but the silence continued. Finally I spoke.

"Brad, you look like a blank wall. Julie's said a real mouthful. Yet you don't even look ruffled."

"Oh, he's ruffled all right," said Julie. "Whenever he gets mad, he clams up and gets that queer look on his face."

"I still don't see what all the fuss is about," insisted Brad. "Julie knows we've got to cut corners, not just now but for the next four years."

"I think she does," I said. "But she's said a lot more than that. In effect, she's said your relationship together is in pretty bad shape. I wish I had an answer for you both."

"Well, tell me," Julie pleaded. "Am I going crazy? Whose fault is it anyway? Why are we like this?" I felt pretty uncomfortable at this point.

"I wish I knew. Julie, I can't tell you or Brad that it's your fault, or his fault. What I can tell you, though, is that from a third party looking on, your marriage seems to need attention. My feeling is that there are some things you need to work on together. The most obvious point to me is that you have lost the note of joy in your marriage. Brad is working a heavy schedule for a very commendable goal—but it really makes him almost a stranger at home. Julie works hard to make ends meet, but without Brad around she loses sight of the reason for doing all of this. Does that sound like a fair comment? It's my impression from your conversation."

"Well," Julie began, "I love my family and I love Brad. That's why I got on that phone and called you."

I waited for Brad to respond. When he didn't. I turned to him. "Well, how about it, Brad. Do you love Julie?"

There were several minutes of silence, which seemed like an hour. Brad looked at Julie and then turned to me. "To be perfectly honest, no." There was a long painful pause. I felt it best not to interrupt.

In tears, now, Julie exclaimed, "*Good grief,* Brad! Things get so bad around here that I call in the minister; you tell us both

that I'm an irresponsible woman when it comes to money; you
don't take any of the blame for our problems and now you say
you don't love me! What's happening to our marriage?" With
that, she disappeared into the kitchen looking for some Kleenex.

Brad looked worried but still said nothing.

"Brad," I asked. "What do you do when Julie keeps after
you?"

"I just don't listen."

Now Julie appeared in the doorway, somewhat composed.

"I can see that," I said. "I feel that you turned her off
several times this evening." Looking at Julie, I continued.
"And I think that sometimes when Brad is about to say
something, Julie, you cut him off. Where we go from here, I
don't know. Both of you are very capable people and I have
every confidence that you can do something about your relationship. Maybe I'm wrong. I really don't know. I'm certain
about this, however; it's going to take both of you to work at
this thing. I think Julie's cry for help and desire to work this
thing out is indication enough, Brad, that she's reaching her
breaking point in terms of living with this thing. Frankly, I
think you both are at a stage where you can prevent a crisis
from getting completely out of control."

Brad spoke. "I know. Look, Arnold, part of the trouble is
that Julie has been saying this same thing for a long time. I
guess when she has gone outside her circle of friends to get
the minister, it is more serious than I thought."

Nodding my agreement, I said, "I think it indicates she's
desperate."

Just then, Julie announced that there was coffee and pie.
We all sat down at the kitchen table. The conversation turned

to talk about the children, about Brad's plans for the university, and lighter matters. I realized, suddenly, that it had grown quite late. While we were all still sitting around the table, I suggested that we join hands in prayer. Afterward, while driving home, I found myself wondering how it would all turn out.

Analysis by WALTER C. JACKSON

This frank and open conversation between Brad and Julie in the presence of a minister displays the agony of their marriage relationship in living color. Money, vocation, personal freedom, relationships to children, and sexual adjustment are all wrapped together in the same package with mistrust, anger, jealousy, loneliness, and frustration. Feelings are under so much pressure that the lifeline of human relations is blocked—communications are seriously curtailed. Neither Brad nor Julie is able to hear what the other really has to say.

Nothing is as important to a married couple as their need to be able to talk with and understand each other. Brad's comments that there isn't *anything new* or that it has all been *said before* are the walls behind which he hides, so he won't have to admit she really is hurt. Her constant way of cutting him off and scolding him as if he were a child renders her unable to hear his hurt, too. No attempt to solve the long list of their problems will be of much help until the important lines of communication are reopened.

However, a Christian friend could do some things to help this couple if he would be willing to share himself and would follow a few simple principles.

First, the would-be helper needs to be aware of his own feelings about the situation. Does he feel pity for Julie, the mistreated wife? Does he feel anger toward Brad, a man with the sensitivity of Fred Flintstone? Or does he reject Julie's outburst believing Brad to be well within his rights? Such feelings will dominate a helper's attitude and interfere unless they are well in mind. A helper does not choose sides in such a way as to promote the conflict and further block communication. His contribution will be to try to make it easier for Brad and Julie to talk to each other. He will maintain friendship for both of them and respond openly to them.

Secondly, the true helper will be aware of his own strengths and weaknesses. There are some things friendship can do; there are also limitations to such a relationship. Attempting to become a diagnostician or a therapist would hinder more than help.

Thirdly, notice that Brad and Julie have responded well to their minister. A friend could encourage them to continue seeing him for counseling, and support any suggestions the minister might make. Such a friend could also consult with the pastor. Together they will be able to make a covenant for prayer and action to be of utmost help to Brad and Julie. Personal interest in their participation in the social, study, and worship life of the church might be of additional help.

Finally, the knowledgeable friend will be aware that if this conversation is any sample, Brad and Julie's life together must be a "hell on earth." The puzzle is that they continue to tolerate it. This may suggest the presence of a more hidden need. A trained counselor or physician could determine the real reasons for this and help them to work through them. The Christian friend will give open affection and support at every moment along the line.

Analysis by JAMES ROBINSON

Jesus said, "The Son of man came not to be ministered unto, but to minister" (Mark 10:45). Therefore, if Christians are to follow their Lord, they must be engaged in ministry to those in need. When trouble comes, to feel compassion is not enough. Some concrete help must be offered. The cases in this volume deal with people who are in trouble. The question that must be answered is, "How can they be ministered unto by Christians?" If the answer to this question can be discovered, it can be applied in other cases of a similar nature.

The approach that has been taken to these case studies is one in which ways to help those in need have been suggested to those who want to minister. No attempt has been made to offer advice to those who find themselves in similar crises situations. The guidelines proposed are for those who desire to help others and not to those who find themselves in need of help.

In each instance an effort has beem made to speak as a pastor to a church member who has become aware of a situation of need and who has come seeking advice on how that need might be met.

Unquestionably, Brad and Julie have a sick marriage. This fact is clear to the objective observer, although it seems to be cloudy for Brad. Whether the marriage can be saved is largely dependent upon the truthfulness of Brad's statement that he does not love Julie. If this is an honest statement of his feelings, then there is little chance that he will be willing to put forth the effort to salvage the marriage. In order for a sick marriage to be made well, there must be mutual love and desire. If Brad does not have this love and desire, the prognosis for the marriage is extremely poor. However, there is a good possibility that Brad has not stated his feelings honestly. Where there is love, there is hope; therefore, Brad and Julie must be given some quick, positive, and practical help.

At a time like this, this young couple needs all of the support which can be given them. They need the support which can be gained from regular church attendance. Obviously, their Christianity has not carried over into their home nor made much of an impact upon their personal lives. Irregular church attendance could be a part of the reason for this. A happily married young couple from Brad and Julie's church needs to be enlisted to visit with them on an appointment basis. An appointment will insure that Brad is at home when the visit is made. Brad and Julie should be appealed to as a couple who is being missed at church rather than as two individuals who are being missed. The visiting couple should be informed of the marital difficulty in the home before making the visit, but no mention of the trouble should be made during the visit.

Brad and Julie need the support of Christian fellowship. The young couple making the initial visit should seek to cultivate a couple-to-couple relationship with Brad and Julie. Being around happily married people strengthens a couple's own marriage. Too, as the relationship develops, opportunity will arise for Brad and Julie to share their problems and for helpful suggestions to be made.

Along with support, this troubled young couple needs wise

counseling. Although their financial problems may be only a symptom of deeper difficulties, they do need some help in this area. Some of the tension over finances could probably be eased with a few simple suggestions such as having Brad go shopping for groceries with Julie occasionally, having Julie keep a running total of her grocery purchases in order to avoid embarrassment at the checkstand, and encouraging Brad to consider the television set and the car as family possessions rather than personal ones. However, even these simple suggestions would carry more weight if they came from a Christian banker to whom the couple had been referred.

If Brad could be led to talk with a physician or professional counselor who could help him see that many of his attitudes are immature and result from his childhood background, this could be extremely beneficial. In many respects he is being selfish and unreasonable. His attitudes put Julie in an almost impossible position. Further marriage counseling is mandatory.

There are other incidental things that can be done to relieve some of the immediate problems. Transportation to the grocery store could be offered Julie, thereby providing not only practical help but also opportunities for making suggestions about shopping and for personal fellowship. Visits could be made by those workers from the church who are responsible for the children. This would help encourage family attendance at church and show Julie that others are interested in her children also.

What Brad ultimately decides about his love for Julie will probably determine the course that this marriage takes. However, Christian friends cannot wait until this decision is made before offering their help. Brad and Julie need it now.

---◆▶---

Analysis by JOHN ISHEE

There are several areas where creative relationships in marriage may be stymied. Frequently, when problems exist in marriage the problems are expressed around the focal points of money, personal ambitions of the marriage partners, unsatisfactory sex relationships, or unsatisfactory relationships with in-laws. Except for the latter problem—that of in-laws—this case study seems to touch upon all of them. It is not unlikely that problems in one of these areas can cause "hangups" in all the other areas. I see in this case study a young couple still striving to develop a style of life that has not emerged since their marriage. One of the key problems is money. He doesn't provide any money for Julie. Perhaps he doesn't have it to provide and is engaged in night school in an effort to better provide for his family. However, financial provisions are only a part of the entire story. In Brad's effort to provide for his own personal ambitions in going to school he has failed to provide for the basic emotional and spiritual needs of his family. Julie feels that she is virtually ignored except when Brad wishes to fulfil his basic sex drive.

One of the things the average church member must recognize is that in the helping process he will encounter persons whose troubles are beyond his capacity and ability to help. He should not be reluctant in seeking special help to meet these problems. In this case, the pastor was the person making the call. If the pastor has had training and experience in marital counseling, he may be able to help Brad and Julie solve some of the basic problems. More often, however, the person who encounters difficulties, such as those being experienced by this couple, will have little experience in dealing with them. Perhaps the greatest ministry that can be provided is to put Brad and Julie in touch with a skilled counselor.

I suspect that money is at the heart of the matter. The Bible says that "the love of money is the root of all evil" (1 Tim. 6:10). In our affluent society, it is equally true that the lack of money can be the root of numerous other evils.

In addition to putting Brad and Julie in touch with specialized help, I would try to lead Brad to see that there are basic needs that need to be met. Perhaps he should make a radical change in his job or his style of life. Certainly, he needs to give Julie more attention and understanding.

Approximately one out of every three marriages end in divorce. Unless some different course is taken, this marriage is destined to end on the rocks. It can still be saved, but it needs special attention and is not able to maintain itself anymore.

"We Did Everything for Him"

Reuben Herring

Not until Jimmy White was in the sixth grade did it occur to his parents that they might have a behavior problem on their hands.

Jimmy was the youngest of five children, and in a way he had been the *pet* of the entire family. He had three older brothers and a sister. The sister was the second oldest child, and the boy nearest Jimmy in age was four years older. All the older children tended to *spoil* Jimmy when he was young.

His parents also made allowances for Jimmy as the youngest child. The other children were made to give in to him and to cater to his whims.

"But you are older than Jimmy," the parents would explain to the other children. "You can't expect him to understand."

Jimmy was full of boyish pranks which his parents regarded indulgently. His mischievousness the other members of the family found rather amusing.

The only problem of any consequence during his early years was that Jimmy liked to "snitch" things. He would pick up items and stuff them into his pockets when he went shopping with his mother, or he would return home from a friend's house with a new toy or some other article. Jimmy's mother would either quietly replace the stolen item or overlook it altogether. She regarded it as the daring behavior characteristic of young boys and not deserving of a reprimand.

During those early years, Mrs. White never regarded her son as a bad boy. He was anything but that. She took him with her regularly to Sunday School and church, where he was well-behaved. She heard his prayers faithfully at night, and they talked at times about God, the church, and the Bible.

"I believe Jimmy is going to be our preacher," she liked to say to her husband with a smile. "You should hear the prayers that boy can say!"

Mr. White was proud of Jimmy, as he was of all his sons. A welder, he followed construction and was seldom at home. Some jobs took him away from home for as long as six months. Even when his work was near their city, he usually was at home only on the weekends. He said often that he wanted his sons "to be men" and liked to assure his friends and neighbors that Jimmy was *all boy*. He reassured his wife when she pointed out that Jimmy frequently brought home things that did not belong to him and then made up stories about how he got them.

"Let the boy grow up," he said. "Boys will be boys—every kid has to snitch a few things to see what he can get away with. Besides, I'd rather have a son who is all boy than a sissy any day."

But that was before Jimmy's sixth-grade teacher called Mrs. White.

"Jimmy is in some rather serious trouble, I'm afraid, Mrs. White," the teacher said bluntly. "Can you and Mr. White come in tomorrow for a conference with the principal?"

"But what is it? What has Jimmy done?" Mrs. White demanded.

"I really can't discuss it over the phone, Mrs. White," the

teacher replied. "But Jimmy has been taking money. Can you and Mr. White come in with Jimmy tomorrow?"

"Well, I'm certain Jimmy hasn't taken any money," Mrs. White answered emphatically. "I most certainly will come in tomorrow, but Mr. White will not be in town again for several days."

In the principal's office the next day Mrs. White found Jimmy's teacher, the principal, Jimmy and three other boys, and the parents of one of the boys.

"I'm sure this is something of a shock for you, Mrs. White," the teacher began. "But Jimmy has been harassing one of the other boys in his class. I caught him in the hall yesterday taking money from Donald here. He has admitted to me that this is not the first time this has happened."

Mrs. White sat and listened in stunned silence as the details were brought out. Jimmy and two of his friends had forced Donald to give them his lunch money. They had done this daily for several weeks and had demanded that Donald bring more money from home. Jimmy had beaten the boy severely the first time he refused to give him money and instructed him to tell his parents that he had suffered the bruises in a fall on the playground.

"Your son has been the ring leader of a reign of terror on the school ground," Donald's mother accused. "Why, our Donnie says your son actually threatened to *kill* him if he told what had been happening."

The Whites found it hard to believe that their son was guilty as charged—so they refused to believe it. They agreed to increase Jimmy's allowance and thereby remove any need for him to take money from other students.

"Little Donnie was probably just scared to death, and his mother was hysterical," Mr. White shrugged off the incident.

"Why, I wish I had a nickel for every fight I got into on the school ground and on the way home."

Jimmy's three older brothers were outstanding athletes in high school and all had been awarded college scholarships on their football ability. Everyone assumed that Jimmy would follow in his brothers' footsteps—particularly Jimmy's father. He made a special effort to get home to see the boys play and saw most of their college games. Mrs. White had collected a voluminous scrapbook of clippings of each of the boys.

"Little Jimmy will show you boys something," Mr. White said proudly to the other boys. "He will do all that you did, only better, and he won't make some of the mistakes you made."

But Jimmy lacked the natural ability of his older brothers. He was sturdily built, but he was not quite as big as the other boys. A more serious handicap was his lack of coordination. He lacked the agility and hand-eye coordination that marks outstanding athletes.

During his first year in high school, Jimmy went out for football—his father would not have heard otherwise. Much was expected of him by everyone—fans, students, players, coaches, and especially his parents. But it soon became apparent to everyone, including Jimmy, that he would never become a star. The natural ability of his brothers just was not there.

Jimmy began to skip practice, to break training regulations, to ignore the instructions of the coaches, and in other ways to goof off. The season was scarcely under way when he was kicked off the squad.

"I have all the patience in the world with a boy who is trying," the coach explained when Mr. White remonstrated with him for cutting his son from the squad. "But Jimmy not only has not tried, he has refused to take instructions. I will not have a boy on my team who does not take instructions or obey the rules. As soon as Jimmy shows me that he wants to play ball and will obey my instructions, I'll consider giving him another chance—but not before then."

"I wasn't kicked off the team—I quit," Jimmy boasted to his friends. "Football is a stupid game anyhow. Why should I take a chance on getting my head split open just so some dumb-head coach can get a new car for having a winning season? Those other dummies can do his dirty work for him if they want to, but not me. Count me out. I know of better ways to get my kicks."

After that Jimmy was regarded by most of his schoolmates as a *hood*—a tough and a troublemaker. He went to the football games and other athletic events and school gatherings, but he went looking for trouble. At the stadium or gym or at some gathering place after the game, he and members of the gang he ran with usually started a fight with boys from rival schools. Failing in this, they picked a fight with members of their own school.

He showed little interest in girls, and they had little to do with him. Most of them were fearful that if they were seen with him his bad reputation would rub off on them. For this reason he was not invited to any private social gatherings. However, this did not prevent Jimmy and his gang from crashing the parties. They usually showed up drunk or feigning drunkenness and tried to start a fight. If no one challenged them, they did their best to disrupt the party and frighten the girls.

One outing which Jimmy and his friends turned into a "rumble" was a cookout at the city park. Just as the party was at its height, Jimmy and three of his pals drove up. They threw sand in the food, poured soft drinks on the campfire, and threatened to throw one of the girls in the lake.

When one of the boys challenged Jimmy, he instructed two of his friends to hold the boy. Jimmy went to the car, returned with a chain, and beat the boy brutally.

As the party poopers drove off, Jimmy snarled at the group, "If any of you fruits say anything about this to anybody—anybody, you hear—we'll kill that creep the next time we catch him."

Jimmy was warned by police the first time he created a disturbance at a game, but after that he was arrested repeatedly for fighting and creating disturbances. Each time, his mother rushed down to the police station and paid the fine or tried to make peace with those who were offended or victimized.

"Jimmy is a good boy," she assured everyone. "He has just gotten in with the wrong crowd. I promise you that this will never happen again."

After each brush with the law, she would have a long talk with Jimmy.

"Son, you have been taught better than this," she would say. "I do wish you would learn to behave like your brothers. They never gave us any trouble like this. I just can't understand what has gotten into you. I have taken you to church and tried to teach you right."

Mr. White was less disturbed. "He's just teed off because he got sacked by the coach," he said. "He'll get it out of his system. Just give him time."

Jimmy went from gang fighting and vandalism to petty theft and burglary. He managed to attend classes often enough to stay in school, but stayed on the borderline between flunking out and being expelled for infractions of

school rules. Finally, in his senior year, he dropped out altogether.

"You are just throwing away your life," his mother warned
and pleaded. "Look at your brothers. All of them went to
college on scholarships and now they have nice jobs. You'll
never amount to anything. No one will hire you these days
without a college education."

"Well, I managed to get along without a college education,"
Jimmy's father put in, "but I did it by hard work. You can suit
yourself about going to college or not, but let me tell you one
thing. You are not going to sit around the house all day on
your dead end and expect me to feed you. You're on your own
now. If you're going to keep putting your feet under my table,
you're going to help put something on it."

A few weeks later, over his mother's protests, Jimmy moved
out of the house and into an apartment with his friends. He
told his mother that he was working at a service station.
Actually he only hung out there during the day. At night he
and his friends operated a burglary ring. They broke into
small neighborhood stores, took what cash they could find,
and cleaned the shelves of goods that could be easily con-
verted into cash. These were stored in the apartment until
they could be disposed of.

It was an exciting life, the profits were good, and Jimmy
and his friends agreed that the "stupid cops" were too busy
knocking down on traffic tickets to chase burglars.

"Besides," they laughed, "you can't beat those hours. We'll
leave the rat race to the jerks who are working their ears off in
college."

Then one night they hit a small drugstore. They had collected the cigarettes, salable drugs, and other merchandise
when they were surprised. The owner of the store had been in

a small room in the back of the store working on the electrical wiring. He came out when he heard noises in the front of the store and caught the burglars at work.

Jimmy and his partner grabbed the man, threw him to the floor, beat him, and left him unconscious as they fled. The owner, a middle-aged man, was hospitalized with a concussion. However, he had recognized one of his assailants and swore out a warrant for Jimmy's arrest.

Again Mrs. White rushed to the police station to bail Jimmy out, but when she discovered that his bond had been set at $10,000, she became hysterical. Then it was pointed out to her that if the drugstore owner died her son would be accused of murder. She collapsed and had to be put to bed.

Mr. White was called home and hired a lawyer. They borrowed money on their home and other possessions to get their son out of jail. Their lawyer recommended that they take Jimmy to a psychiatrist, but the Whites hesitated. The issue was settled when Jimmy flatly refused to see "any head shrinker."

The store owner recovered, but the Whites' lawyer held out little hope that Jimmy would escape a jail sentence. He pointed out that the judge might not be lenient when he looked over their son's long record of law violations.

The judge did sentence Jimmy to a prison term, but suspended the sentence and placed Jimmy in the custody of his father. The court instructed Mr. White to arrange his business affairs so that he could be at home with his son and could check daily on his whereabouts. Jimmy was advised either to enrol in school full time or to find employment that met the approval of the court.

"I just don't understand it," Jimmy's mother said to her friends afterward. "We brought up Jimmy just like we did the other boys, and his brothers never gave us a minute's trouble, not a bit. We did our best to bring him up right—took him to church and taught him to pray and everything. If I was an unfit mother or something like that, I could understand it. But we did everything we knew to do for him. I just don't understand it."

———◆———

Analysis by WALTER C. JACKSON

Jimmy White is the kind of child seen all too frequently in our juvenile and criminal courts: young, defended by over-protective parents, a life-style of disregard for the rights and property of others, and a contempt and gross disregard for the law and its enforcement officers.

This story of Jimmy's growth and development suggests some lessons to be remembered about the rearing of children. An environment of trust, understanding, love, and protection is needed by the growing child; but discipline and authority regarding the rights, privileges, and property of others are also necessary. The absence of such discipline and authority in Jimmy's life helped make him incapable of living in the adult world.

Also in focus here is the truth that outward conformity to parents' routines of Sunday School, worship attendance, or religious group activities is no assurance that a child is being "good." Even proficiency in religious rituals like prayer and Bible study are not guarantees that a child's personality is developing normally. A child may see these kinds of behavior as ways to keep his parents "off his back" or to give God his daily instructions about how to operate some corner of his universe.

The Whites need help. They need an understanding friend to tell them they have not yet seen Jimmy as he really is. Somehow, they need to be able to see that their relationship to Jimmy has not really changed: they are still defending him as the sweet little child who can do no harm in the face of all kinds of authority. This friend could also suggest that they consult a family counseling service staffed by competent professionals to sort out their own responsibility in Jimmy's predicament, and to receive insight and direction for self-growth as well as for their relationship with Jimmy.

The Whites need to find ways to communicate to Jimmy that their love for him has not changed but that his behavior is quite unacceptable. Remedial work to help Jimmy learn the lessons of life required to prepare him for adult responsibility should be begun. Friends and family will need to present a united front to Jimmy, rewarding him when he respects the rights of others, requiring him to accept responsibility and to pay the penalties for unacceptable acts.

Jimmy also needs professional help. This should not be optional at this stage! The story as recorded here does not reflect Jimmy's responses to his parents and other authority figures. Open anger and hostility toward authority persons at this age is serious but may well be more related to immaturity. If his characteristic responses are calculated to appease and manipulate, then illness is a more serious possibility. The various therapies employed by the selected professional should be supported by the entire White family. Friends should be especially sensitive to the need of Jimmy's parents for supportive attention.

An alert pastor will be prepared for the response of guilt and depression on the part of the Whites as Jimmy enters rehabilitative therapy. Here the gospel is most needed. Perhaps a suitable group within the church could supply the time when they can share the agony of their experience and expound on the lessons they have learned. Many of the things which happened to Jimmy are part of the experience of almost every child. Sharing the truth of what happens when "spoiling" a child persists into late adolescence may be a time of mutual sharing and confession for many parents and become a basic ingredient in a ministry of reconciliation for the Whites.

Analysis by JAMES ROBINSON

Mrs. White's statement that she does not understand the reason for her son's behavior provides a good starting place in the attempt to minister to this family in need. She should be helped to see that the reason for his failure lies not in lack of love but in lack of wisdom. She should be led to understand that taking a child to church and teaching him to pray is not enough to insure his success in life.

To the objective observer, several parental mistakes on the part of the Whites are obvious. They catered to all of Jimmy's whims when he was small and allowed the other children to do so. They did not see him as an individual who should be allowed to live up to his own desires and capabilities, but rather sought to mold him into the shape of his older brothers who were entirely different from him. The Whites protected their son from all of the consequences of his anti-social behavior and sought to rationalize it rather than facing up to its reality and allowing their son to suffer for wrongs done.

The reason for helping Mrs. White understand her son's actions is that her past mistakes might not be repeated in the future. Apparently, she tried her best to raise her son properly. There is no need to make her feel guilty over the past. However, she does need to avoid the continuation of past errors. Perhaps a kind Christian woman near her own age could aid her in her search for understanding.

Mr. White also needs the help of Christian friends. He needs to be supported as he bears the burden of his son's criminal activity and as he seeks to offer guidance to Jimmy in the future. He may need some immediate help in changing jobs in order to adequately supervise his son. Men from the church who are in a position to do so can help him in his search for a new position. They can establish a friendship with him and invite him to become active in the church now that he will be at home more. A change in jobs and in friends may help Mr. White to see that manliness is not to be equated with athletic prowess, fighting, and rowdy conduct.

In the effort to help the White family, Jimmy himself must not be forgotten. He has an immediate decision to make, and he will likely need some help in making it. A conference could be set up with an understanding school administrator who would be able to offer some sound advice on whether Jimmy should return to school or get a job. If the decision reached is that Jimmy should go to work, then help should be offered in finding a suitable position. A member of the church who personally understands Jimmy's need might extend a job offer so that not only could a position be secured but an opportunity gained for future help and guidance.

Jimmy's probationary status is going to make it mandatory

that he secure new friends. He will need adult friends who know his past but are willing to help him make the future different.

He will need friends his own age who will seek to make him welcome in a new environment. His fellow Christians ought to seek to provide this friendship.

It would be most helpful if after gaining his confidence, one of his Christian friends suggested that Jimmy get some professional counseling. He should be helped to see that such counseling is not needed because he is mentally ill but rather to help him avoid in the future some of the trouble he has had in the past. Such counseling might ultimately include Jimmy's parents as well.

Jimmy's parents did not do everything for him. They left much to be done by others who are concerned enough to minister.

———◆———

Analysis by JOHN ISHEE

I firmly believe that the biblical injunction "Train up a child in the way he should go: and when he is old, he will not depart from it" (Prov. 22:6), is true. Sometimes, however, in our efforts to do one thing, we unconsciously do another. Our perceptions of what we are doing are viewed quite differently by the child. Although there is not agreement on how parents should relate to their children, I see several principles being ignored or violated in this case study.

First, children must be prepared to face the realities of life. In this case study, I see parents being overprotective of a child and thus failing to equip him both emotionally and intellectually for dealing with the realities of life. By their own admission, they did everything for him. As a child grows physically, he should also be assisted—at least allowed—to grow in responsible independence.

Second, genuine love for children is sometimes expressed through discipline. Parents who care little for their children are sometimes the ones who allow them excessive amounts of liberty in their daily routines. While some people may interpret such activity as expressions of love, I more often think of them in terms of expressions of irresponsibility. The failure to correct Jimmy for his misdemeanor—bringing little items home that did not belong to him—allowed the behavior to grow into more serious acts of vandalism.

Third, each child must be allowed to be himself as he grows up. I was particularly troubled by the parents' actions as they compared Jimmy with his three older brothers. They set their high expectations for Jimmy and perhaps caused a great deal of inner turmoil and frustration in Jimmy's life. Maybe this frustration expressed itself in acts of vandalism and repudiation of authority.

I highly suspect that Jimmy's patterns of life have been so established that he will need psychiatric help to overcome some of his problems.

Regular attendance at church and the understanding of the community of Christian fellowship could provide Jimmy with some of the social reinforcement he needs to make adequate changes.

"What Happened to All the Money?"

Michael L. Speer

With eyes dancing as only those of a seven-year-old can, Teddy held the red toy fire engine toward his mother and asked, "Mother, may I have this? Oh, please, Mother, may I?"

Even through the plastic bag the red of the fire engine seemed to clash with Teddy's normally red hair and made it carrot orange in comparison.

Martha looked at her son, but her concentration was elsewhere. She really didn't see or hear until he pleaded again.

"Can I, Mother, please? It's only 79¢."

"No, Teddy, not this time. We don't have enough money," she answered mechanically. She couldn't help but wonder why supermarkets had to have those attractive displays at the end of each aisle, that would attract the attention of adults as well as children.

Teddy's eyes stopped dancing and suddenly turned to brown pebbles in pools of water.

"That's all you ever say," he exclaimed. "We never have enough money for anything any more!"

Almost as quickly as he had picked the toy off the hanger on the display rack and carried it to his mother, he now retraced his steps and hung the desirable fire engine among the maze of other toys. A single tear found its way down each cheek, but he didn't actually cry. He simply dropped his chin to his chest and fell in step behind his mother without another word.

Somehow Martha wished he would cry—would throw a fit that would make her angry. It was easier to say no at such times like that. His sudden outburst and ultimate acceptance of "we don't have enough money" seemed to hurt her far more than if he had protested actively.

Martha looked at the piece of round steak she was holding. It seemed like the price had doubled in the last few months! She put it back in place and carefully selected the cheaper cut of chuck roast and a pound of hamburger meat. Maybe with enough vegetables she could get two meals out of the roast, she thought, and the ground meat would have to replace the usual cubes of beef in the vegetable soup.

Quickly, Martha pushed the grocery cart down the aisle past the delicious frozen desserts and ice cream treats. She dreaded Teddy's next request—but none came. He just followed silently along behind to the check-out counter.

Martha took the items from the grocery cart one by one and mentally added the cost again as she placed them on the conveyer. I hope I have enough money, she thought as she remembered the embarrassment of not having enough the time before and having to ask the clerk to return one item. She had tried to act nonchalant about the whole thing, saying something funny about "Frank must have been in the grocery money again—I can't seem to find that other five-dollar bill." But it wasn't funny and she knew her real embarrassment showed through.

"Eighteen eighty-seven with the tax," the clerk said as he rang up the final total.

Martha handed him the two ten-dollar bills and was

tempted to send Teddy back for the fire engine, but being realistic about it she did nothing.

Leaving the store, she felt a chill in the early October afternoon. The trees were still covered with multicolored leaves, but she knew only too well that they would soon be bare. This only helped to remind her that Caroline needed a new winter coat, and she wished that she had bought it last spring when they were on sale. Things were better then, financially, but she hadn't anticipated the sudden change of events.

Traffic was light. She was ahead of the late afternoon rush and the trip from the shopping center to their home took only a few minutes. When she arrived, Caroline had finished her homework and was playing some of her last year's pieces on the piano. She was eleven and had taken lessons for three years and really enjoyed them. There had never been the coaxing or threatening to get her to practice that usually accompanied such lessons.

Caroline followed as Martha carried the bags of groceries into the kitchen and set them on the table.

"Mother," she quizzed, "when can I start taking piano lessons again?"

She had stopped taking the lessons when school was out in June. Martha had realized then that it would be necessary. However, rather than try to explain the financial difficulties to the children, she had simply told Caroline that she thought a summer of vacation from the lessons would be more enjoyable. They had always tried not to worry the children with financial problems.

"Perhaps you can start again before long, dear. We'll see," Martha said.

"But I thought you were going to let me begin again when school started," Caroline moaned.

"Let's not talk about it right now." Martha tried to sound cheerful, but it was a feeble attempt. "Run along and play while I get supper. Daddy will be home before long."

Martha tried to occupy her mind with preparing supper but she found difficulty escaping the reality of their money problems. Teddy's frank exclamation, "We never have enough money for anything anymore!" pretty well summed up the situation.

Frank had had a good job with a major manufacturing company. In fact, he had been the head man in the product design department of the international office. But last January the company president had died. In the ensuing shuffle for higher positions, Frank's immediate supervisor, one of the company vice presidents, had lost out to a younger man who was a personal friend of the new president. Of course the changes didn't stop with the "top brass." Each man seemed to have friends of his own whom he wanted working with him. Frank had always avoided political entanglements and tried only to achieve success through his ability to produce. He thought his job was pretty secure, but ability wasn't enough this time. On May 15, Frank had gotten a notice that he was being transferred to a similar department at the local plant. Fortunately, he was made the head of the department and didn't take a cut in salary, but neither did he get the $95 a month raise which he would have received in just six weeks as he began his seventh year with the company and his third year in the international office.

"I'm sorry to have to do this, Frank," the new boss had explained when he told him about the transfer, "but I've worked with Ted Brannham for years and we're sort of a team. I know this position won't give you the raise you had anticipated, but we will keep the salary the same this year and perhaps the position can be reevaluated later. You will be at the top of the pay scale as the head of the department and the benefits will be the same except that you won't have the stock options."

The stock options really didn't matter much. Frank had never been able to take advantage of the plan for purchasing up to $600 worth of company stock each year at a reduced rate. He had always passed it by, thinking that he would take advantage of it the following year when he got his raise. However, whenever any raise came, it seemed that it was always needed for other commitments. This year's raise, although it had still been six weeks away, had already been counted on in the family budget.

Martha had a serious bone disease and the doctor had insisted that they move from their split-level home into a one-floor plan so she wouldn't have to climb stairs. They had bought their old house seven years before and had a low 5¼ percent interest rate. The thought of selling and buying another house had been difficult to accept, but finally they were able to work with a contractor who took their old house in on one of his brand new one-floor models. It was a beautiful home in a lovely neighborhood. But the interest rate was 8½ percent and, of course, both taxes and insurance were higher on the more expensive house. All in all, it had increased their house payment $57 a month. The moving had been an additional cost, and Martha had insisted on new drapes and curtains. Some of the old furniture just didn't fit into the new house and had had to be replaced. Besides, Frank's raise had only been three months away then and both the furniture company and the department store where they had bought the drapes and curtains had allowed 45 days before the first payments came due. That meant that actually only one payment would be due before the $95 a month raise. All in all they were actually going to come out a little ahead each month. After the raise! But that was six months ago.

Martha heard the car pull up in front of the house and watched as Frank got out and waved good-bye to the other men. She knew he hated riding in a car pool, but it was more economical this way. Frank only drove one week each month, and that cut down on gas and repair bills. It also gave her the car when she had to have it for trips to the doctor and shopping. Frank stopped to pet Lady as she wagged her tail in greeting, then came into the house.

"I'm home," he called as he walked in. He seemed to be in a good mood which in itself was unusual anymore. Martha was glad. She knew they had to have a serious talk about the bills, but first she hoped they could have a nice supper and a pleasant time with the children before they put them to bed.

Things did go well that evening. The supper was good, and after supper Frank played with the children in the backyard for a while and then they watched TV until it was time for their baths and bed.

When the children were settled, Frank read the paper, then finally asked the inevitable question, "Did we get any mail today?"

Martha burst into tears! She couldn't help it. She had worried constantly for weeks, and now it seemed as though she couldn't stand it any longer.

"Yes, we got mail," she sobbed. "More bills! Oh, Frank, what will we do?" She cried as she ran to the bathroom for a Kleenex.

She was more composed when she came back.

"What did we get today?" Frank asked. He looked tired and Martha knew all this placed just as much strain on him as it did on her. He knew the lesser position was a result of company politics, but just the same he felt the embarrassment of the change in positions.

"Well," Martha hesitated, "we got the dentist bill from when Teddy fell and broke his tooth last month, and we got a reminder that the semi-annual payment on the car insurance is due. I don't know how I had forgotten it, but with everything else on my mind I just hadn't realized that it was that time again. But that's not the worst," she hesitated and started to cry again. "Oh, Frank, what are we going to do? The electric company sent us a statement with a notice that if we don't pay our bill they will cut off our electricity!"

Frank's heart sank. "Don't cry, sweetheart," he consoled. "We'll work through this somehow. I guess we should have taken a lesson from the people in the Bible who put away some resources during the fat years to have in store during the lean years. But Mother and Dad never did, and I guess I just didn't learn the value of it. 'We always seem to have just exactly enough bills to take all my salary no matter what we buy or don't buy,' Dad used to say. Maybe then it wasn't nearly so easy to buy anything you wanted and pay for it later."

Frank and Martha had received several credit cards they hadn't asked for. They hadn't planned to use them at first, but soon found how convenient it was to carry the cards rather than cash or writing so many checks. And since one of them could be used at so many different places, it made it even more convenient. The 1½ percent per month interest on the unpaid balance really didn't seem like much. It wasn't until the "truth-in-lending" law went into effect that they realized they had been paying the equivalent of 18 percent per year. By that time the bills were far beyond what they had intended to spend, and the monthly payments represented a large part of Frank's monthly salary.

"How much is the electric bill?" Frank asked.

"Fifty-seven dollars," Martha answered. "I haven't paid it for three months. I kept thinking that things would get better, but there just isn't enough money to go around. I have cut way down on groceries, I've been spot cleaning and pressing your suits myself, and I haven't had my hair done for almost four months. But all of that still isn't nearly enough. Things would have been fine if you had gotten the raise, but . . ." Martha stopped abruptly. She hadn't meant to mention the raise again. She knew Frank felt badly enough about it anyway, and after all the bills were largely her fault.

"Well," Frank took up the conversation, "we didn't have any way of knowing what was going to happen, but I guess we should have held off on some of our purchases until we had the cash in hand or at least until I definitely had the raise. We can't help that now. All we can do is take a good look at what we owe and see what we can do about it. Don't cry, honey, we'll work this thing out someway." But deep inside, Frank realized that he really didn't know what they were going to do.

Analysis by WALTER C. JACKSON

Shortage of money in the face of modern living is a constant problem in twentieth-century America. Every year another several items once considered luxuries are added to the "basic need" list of middle-class households. Frank and Martha have had the classic problem of money shortage compounded by unavoidable medical needs and an unexpected business reverse. Their situation is serious in their present state of affairs, but it could become more critical. Increased or added illness, another reorganization at the plant, or trouble from another quarter could bring this family to bankruptcy, not to mention the severe mental and emotional scars such a crisis could inflict.

Those moved to be of special help to this family have a variety of needs to which they may respond. The most obvious is their economic situation. Apparently, Frank and Martha have handled their monthly obligations somewhat casually and hold periodic tear-filled scenes like the one described. They seem to be exhausting most of their energy trying to convince themselves, if not everyone else, that their life is just "business as usual." They appear to have kept alive the myth that if they just take a few superficial measures, the whole problem will vanish.

Hopefully, they will share some of their hurt with a knowledgeable friend, pastor, or professional person. He will point out the need to accept the gravity of the situation and arrange for Frank and Martha to confront each other and their situation as a problem to be worked and solved, not swept under the rug. Obviously, some hard decisions for economy—like the return of recently purchased goods—or change in their life style—like omitting some additional luxuries—will be necessary. These will have to be made under conditions of open communication and be sufficient to remedy the economic pressure. In the event that they insist on doing it alone, resources like Robert Hasting's book, *How to Manage Your Money* or the "Complete Money Management Institute Library" published by the Household Finance Corporation, would be helpful. (See Resources.)

Another area of need concerns their feelings about their predicament. Martha may feel guilty that her illness has caused extra financial strain; Frank may feel guilty because he has not been able to provide enough money to support his family in their accustomed manner. Someone who helps them express these feelings openly and provides a climate where grace and forgiveness can be experienced will be a friend indeed.

Frank's hidden anger about his job should be recognized and accepted in open discussion. A friend could challenge his rigidity in offering only his ability to produce. This may signify a basic unwillingness to share himself in the camaraderie of the marketplace or it may reveal the basic loneliness of his style of life. His unwillingness to compete might suggest the wisdom of moving to a different place of employment.

The barrenness of the family life and the isolation of the children appear also as areas of need. The ministry of the church to the religious, social, and personal needs of this family could make the difference between existence and fulness of life. At least, a caring pastor could be called to be the catalyst for personal and community care.

Analysis by JAMES M. ROBINSON

This crisis situation offers an opportunity for Christians to engage both in an immediate ministry and an extended one. Frank and Martha need immediate help with their electric bill and insurance payments on their car. To arrange a loan to meet these payments would alleviate their acute problem but would add to their chronic difficulty. These bills could be paid by the church without embarrassing the couple simply by sending checks to the electric company and to the insurance agency. Frank and Martha do not even need to know necessarily who paid the bills.

After the immediate need has been met, some attention must be given to their general problem of financial difficulty. They are victims of circumstance to a degree, but their trouble has been greatly intensified by poor planning and by unwise use of available money. To spot the lack of wisdom in making commitments to be met from a raise that is not yet a reality is not difficult. Neither is it hard to see that every family needs some sort of savings plan. However, not only do Frank and Martha need some understanding as to how their problem developed, but they also need some advice as to how to work their way out of their trouble. The person to offer counseling to them along this line is not just the average church member but someone who has had wide financial experience. Most churches either have such a person within their membership or have access to a Christian banker. Frank and Martha need to talk with such a man. He could offer to them invaluable advice. To arrange such a conference for them, with their approval, would be an act of ministry.

Both Frank and Martha need friendship and understanding during this time of trouble. A Christian friend could provide a listening ear for Martha. She obviously needs someone besides Frank with whom to share her problems. Perhaps this friend could help her understand the need for being honest with the children about the financial status of the family. Children have a way of accepting the situation as it is and adjusting to it. For Martha to keep making excuses to her children is for her to run the risk of causing them to lose confidence in her. Martha also needs to be honest with herself. All of the problem has not occurred because Frank did not get his raise. A loving husband will try his best to provide for his wife's desires. Therefore, the wife must be careful about her demands. A Christian friend might seek to interject a positive note by pointing out that even in the midst of difficulty, Martha has the blessings of a fine husband and healthy children.

Frank needs to have his ego lifted. He, too, needs a Christian friend to whom he can pour out his feelings of failure and resentment. He cannot do this to his wife, because he feels that she has enough problems of her own and that he must be the strong one in this difficult time. This would be an excellent time for Frank to be offered a job at the church so that he will feel needed and wanted. Just to have someone convey the presence of concern and understanding would be helpful to him.

Frank and Martha will not work out of their difficulty in just a few weeks. They need ministry now, and they are going to keep on needing it for an extended period. They must be handled carefully so that their pride and dignity might be maintained. However, the proper care and concern will not only help them, but it will also cause them to love their church and glorify their heavenly Father.

Analysis by JOHN ISHEE

Frank reminds me so much of the individual referred to by William H. Whyte, Jr., in *The Organization Man*. He is caught in the struggle of trying to balance his personal and family wishes and his career. He has placed a great deal of faith in his organization only to be disappointed by an unforeseeable event.

Certainly Frank and his family have had their difficulties. Martha's illness has undoubtedly taken a great deal of money. However, most corporations make it possible for people like Frank to carry insurance to cover a great deal of the cost. I suspect, therefore, that illness has not caused a major financial drain from the budget.

In looking at the difficulties faced by this family, one may overlook some of the basic principles that were violated as they managed their money.

First, it is not a good idea to spend your money until you actually get it. The violation of this principle led the family into a budgetary crisis. Granted that Martha needed the one-story house because of her illness. But would it not be possible to hold out a little longer until they were sure that Frank would get his raise? Couldn't the family "pitch in" and assist the mother with some of the household duties, especially those that needed to be performed on the second floor?

Second, I believe children should be included in the financial matters of the family. There are two extremes to be avoided. First, it is not a good idea to always be talking about how broke the family is. Children sometimes get the idea that they are living in poverty when actually they are not. When the parents say "We don't have the money to buy that," it should be said within a context that has been explained. The context is that while the money might be gathered to buy a particular object, the value system of the family has led them to spend the money in another way. Actually, few people have all the money they need to buy all the items they want. Of necessity, they must express value judgments which lead them to buy certain items and omit others. Therefore, children should be apprised of the fact that money is not available to buy all the things they want. The other extreme is to say nothing to the children about the amount of money that exists within the family. Inevitably, this leads to misrepresenting the truth when the children ask for certain items. Frank and Martha did this with their daughter who wanted to take piano lessons. Rather than saying that money was not available for lessons at that particular time, they insisted on telling their child that it would be a good idea for her to take a vacation from taking piano. Such statements are not good, simply because they are not true. I believe it is a good idea to be honest with children regarding money matters. When money is not available for a particular item, the parents should say so, explaining the fact that the situation may not always be that way. People do get over financial crisis.

Third, the amount of money a family earns is not always a good indicator of how stable their finances are. Certainly, the family that lives in the ghetto and has a very meager income has chronic financial problems. But, in some cases, so do the junior executives who are striving to attain a standard of living that is beyond their means. When Frank was head of the product design department, did he feel that he had to play a certain status role? Who are Frank and Martha's friends? Do their friends set their style of life? Are they trying to live in an "economic class" that is beyond their means?

I highly suspect that several things could be done to put the family's finances on a sound basis. Many cities have service agencies that provide help for families in how to overcome dire financial trouble.

Finally, let me say that it is very easy to sympathize with

Frank and Martha. What young couple raising a family has not experienced some financial difficulty? Inevitably, it seems to be a part of life. Therefore, in trying to help this couple, I would not want to overmagnify the problems they face. Many of them are very common to young Americans raising a family in the twentieth century.

"Everything Seems Like Such a Loss"

Frank Grayum

"Now to get settled down to some business," thought Walter, as the huge jet aircraft taxied to a full stop in front of Gate 14 at International Airport. It had been a good but very long flight and now the activity for which he came must get underway. Not having luggage along to bother him, Walter made his way directly to the cabstand and was soon riding along the freeway to the downtown motor inn. He tried to remember the important parts of conversation he and his supervisor had discussed before leaving the office. Most of the details were clear in his mind, but some things he felt to be important were rather vague. He began to feel ill-prepared for the coming business engagement. This condition of uneasiness caused the hurried pace and the noise of the traffic to go almost unnoticed.

The abrupt stop of the cab in front of the motor inn caught Walter by complete surprise. Momentarily his mind had wandered in anticipation of the business deal, but now the reality of the long hot ride was upon him. He made his way to the front desk and asked the desk clerk to make change for a twenty-dollar bill. After paying the cab driver, he checked in to his room. After settling in the room, he went to the coffee shop for a quiet dinner.

Upon finishing his meal, he returned to his room for a review of some basic information that would be necessary to know before meeting with the prospective client. As he looked through his attaché case, some papers he needed were not there. As he tried to recall this information to mind, he began to realize that in the last few months he had not been at any of the decisive company board meetings. He had not even been invited to them. He knew well enough what was generally going on in the business, but now he felt uneasy and uninformed about future detailed planning. The business was a large firm and in a very short time had grown from infancy to be a giant in the field of industry. He thought of the many promising young executives that were now occupying the important positions around the conference tables. They were sitting where he once sat. Now they were the ones making the key decisions concerning the company's future. He thought how the labor force had changed and a seemingly higher quality people were producing a higher quality product. Recalling all this to mind led him to see that even this business engagement was not very important, and if he was unable to sign the contract, the company would never miss the small amount of business. The preceding moments had been extremely painful and led Walter to anticipate his future with the company.

As all this flashed through his mind, he felt the need to talk with his wife. She had always been a help to him in crisis situations, and he was needing to talk to someone now. He lifted the receiver on the telephone and placed a long distance call with the operator at the front desk. Unable to reach his wife, he asked the operator to keep placing the call until he was able to reach her.

In the next few minutes, a strange loneliness, an uncertain

sick feeling came over him. Many things that had occurred in earlier years began to flash back into his mind. He began to think about the good old days when he was a company leader. He had made many important decisions and had given guidance to the business. He began to doubt the wisdom and experience of those men who were now leading out in the company. He felt that they were too young to make such important strides as quickly as they were doing. He began to get angry, thinking of how they had stepped in and taken over. In fact, he resented them all together.

For instance, there was Burson. He was a constant threat to the company's image. After all, the company was noted for its stability and success through the past few years. And along came a young fellow that didn't fit the traditional mold of a professional. Long hair, fancy pants, and shirts with ruffles just wasn't the "rock of Gibraltar" image. Why, he even dared to speak out in committee meetings against the accepted patterns of the past. That Burson! What a young, outspoken whippersnapper.

And then there was Jones. That "know-it-all." He seemed to think that everyone ought to come to him for ideas. He sat up there in that big office and just couldn't wait to tell someone about his latest brilliant brainstorm. Why, just the other day he turned back some excellent promotional emphasis for the company's public relations. If he just had a little more experience he would learn that he didn't know so much after all.

"What about that recent promotion that should have been mine! Why did they bring in an outsider who knew nothing about the business? I could easily have moved into that position. All that seems important anymore is to have a long string of academic degrees behind your name. Experience seems to count for nothing. He even makes more money than me and does a lot less work. If I didn't help him with that paper work he would never be able to put on the front that he does. Most of the credit he gets really belongs to me. He really is an okay guy, but I can't stand him because of what the company has done to me."

All this thinking caused him to see that even though he was near retirement, he had actually accomplished very little with his life. "What has it all been for?" he thought. He had given his life for the company cause, and now it seemed to be going down the drain. All the big plans he had had in the beginning were never really realized. Even those plans in his personal life were still in the future and he feared that they too would never become a reality. He thought of the house where they now lived. It was much smaller than what he had hoped for. They had always worked for their "dream house" and now it looked like it was just going to continue to be a dream. He still had to buy things on credit and his savings amounted to a lot less than he liked to think about. It seemed like every time he almost made it through one crisis, another would arise; it would take all his savings just to pay the bills. "Everything seems like such a loss," he thought to himself. "Especially when I talk about money." But after all, you can't live without money and you have to make every dollar you can. "Maybe that's my problem, I sought only for the material things in life."

He was thankful, however, for one thing. His wife had always stayed by him through thick and thin. She had supported him through it all. She had always given him full support in whatever he felt like he needed to do. Her support had helped him through many tight situations. But somehow he felt like he had never lived up to her expectations.

Right now life seemed to be closing in all around him and he was going no where but down.

But then there were his two fine sons. What about them! They were his pride and joy. They both were very successful by traditional standards and had very fine homes. His youngest was in his last semester of graduate school and would soon receive his Ph.D. degree. But what lasting relationship had he established with them? They certainly never listened to his advice, and he felt like they ignored his counsel altogether. He felt like both of them considered him a failure since he had never reached the top. But they just didn't understand! Fate had been against him. He had not had the opportunity for an education that he had provided for them. All of their education was at his expense. And now they acted as if they didn't even appreciate his efforts to provide it for them.

"What really upsets me is the paradox of John. John and I started out with the company the very same day. Our abilities were almost equal. I did outshine him in most areas but not overwhelmingly so. He did seem to excel in one area. He has always been able to get along with people and especially important people. He always meets the right guys, always knows the right connections, and always gets the important assignment. And after all, you have to get the big assignment to go to high places. But it was his tactics and business ethics that I disapprove of. I would never polish an apple for anyone! John seems to delight in the activity whenever the opportunity comes along." He thought, "Oh well, I'm glad I'm not like that. I guess that my whole problem is that I chose a vocation too quickly." You know, it was at John's suggestion that I join the firm when I really didn't want to. But after a few months it just seemed too embarrassing to get out. I always felt like there was something greater for me to do than to spend my life in an office. But what would it have been? That I didn't know.

Suddenly he was brought back to reality by the ringing of the telephone. The operator told him that she was unable to complete his call as requested but that she would keep trying. Walter told her to forget it, that she need not keep trying. He felt too depressed to talk to even his wife at the moment.

After a few short minutes, preparing to go to bed and get some sleep, Walter wondered if he would ever pull out of this crisis situation. What does tomorrow hold? Only tomorrow knows.

Analysis by WALTER C. JACKSON

This story is an illustration of a middle-age depression. Having arrived at what he felt would be the greatest period of his life, a man sees the world passing him by. In response, he becomes depressed.

Walter's depression grows out of the fact that he has failed to differentiate between *who he is* and *what he does*. If one of his ideas is rejected, he feels personally rejected. If one of his projects fails, he feels that he personally, and not the project, has failed. With enough failures coupled with an absence of reward and promotion, his depressed feelings are aggravated.

A typically power-oriented man, Walter feels powerless. He has few of the symbols of power: money, influence, position, conquest. He feels he has failed his wife and is not even free to rejoice in the accomplishments of his sons. He is really quite angry about all this and quite alone.

Walter's basic need in this situation is for a warm friend

and genuine affection. Walter needs someone he can trust, a friend who will listen and understand when he expresses his deepest feelings. This friend will not change the subject by sharing his own feelings of anger about some other situation but will help Walter concentrate on his own. The friend will be able to accept the intense anger and would say something like, "You're really angry, and I think I see why you are." Walter will be free then to "let it all hang out," and the friend will take whatever time necessary to listen to everything.

When the fury of the anger is over, it will be time to see what can be learned. Why are so many of his hostile feelings focused on younger men and their successes? What part in the whole process can be caused by the fact that Walter is growing older, his body is less vigorous, his energies not able to match his dreams. What kinds of limitations will he have to accept because of age which hinder him but do not affect his youthful competitors? Is he really willing to deal creatively with this problem instead of allowing his anger to make him continually less effective?

A good friend could help him to see his many accomplishments instead of only his failures. He will help him to begin the process of identifying the several different things he could do to come to terms with himself and his lot in life.

Is finding another job a real possibility; does he really feel so much a part of his company he does not want to leave? How can he handle his feelings in such a way as to contribute what he can to the business? What other interests of religious, civic, social, or leisure activity could he move toward, especially those which would continue after retirement?

More important than this problem-solving process, the friend will insist that Walter reappraise his family situation. He will encourage him to catch up with the warm feelings of

love and affection shared with his wife and sons; to see that
here he already has some of the greatest values life can offer.
The friend will also encourage him to reclaim his faith in God
or lead him to find it; to lead him to discover that the love and
forgiveness of God in Jesus Christ is freely given no matter
what a man thinks himself to be or has accomplished in life
and business.

--------◆▶------

Analysis by JAMES ROBINSON

Walter has come to that time of life that all experience who
live long enough. This is the time when the realization dawns
that the future has mostly become the past. This is a difficult
time for anyone. Some very real adjustments must be made.
The time for dreaming has gone, and the time for facing
reality has arrived.

Walter feels that he is an unimportant failure who has been
unjustly treated by life. He needs someone who is willing to
listen as he expresses his resentment. Many times the free and
open expression of resentment will cause the resentment to
lessen. Apparently Walter does not actually resent the
younger men with whom he is working. He even seems to
grudgingly admit some respect for their abilities. His hostility
is directed mostly at his company and is caused by his feeling
that the company has not dealt fairly with him. If he can be
led to actually express this feeling, he may be helped to see
that the company has not singled him out for injustice. He is
experiencing the typical syndrome of one who is beginning to
see time and progress remove him from where the action is.

Walter's need is to feel needed. His company genuinely
does need him if only he can be led to realize this. The young

men in a company can supply energy and creativity. Their enthusiasm is needed as well as their optimism. However, they need the wisdom and the conservatism that can only be supplied by the more mature employee. Walter knows that he is helping his younger colleagues; but rather than seeing this as a contribution which he is making to his company, he sees it as a case of being used by the younger men.

In all probability, Walter is losing some of his effectiveness. Most people do as they grow older. His company is wisely taking some of his former responsibilities from him. Less responsibility, however, will give him more time for a hobby or an avocation that will provide both recreation and a new interest. It would be an act of love to try to get him started in some activity which would make him appreciate the opportunity to so engage himself. A civic or church responsibility might be found for him which would help him to take his eyes off the past and look more to the future.

A phone call to Walter's sons could be tremendously helpful. They could do a great deal for him simply by understanding his need for encouragement and appreciation and expressing these to him. No doubt their appreciation and gratitude for their father is deep. Certainly, they would prefer a father who had maintained his self-respect and enjoyed limited accomplishment to one who had sacrificed his self-respect and accomplished more. At this time in his life, their father needs them just as they needed him in their younger years. They can help him see and major upon his successes in life rather than his failures. They can help him count his blessings rather than his losses.

The easy way out is to say that Walter's feelings are fairly normal for a man his age and, therefore, do not need to be taken too seriously. The suggestion could be made that time will take care of things and Walter will be all right. Yet, Walter is hurting. He cannot see the promise of the future because of the gloom of the past and present. Concerned Christians cannot simply stand by and watch him suffer. Walter needs someone who is willing to weep with him while he is weeping in order that the time may come when that one can rejoice with him as he is rejoicing.

------◆------

Analysis by JOHN ISHEE

The description of Walter reminds me of some people I know. Walter has several problems.

The first problem is what I call "Lot's wife complex." Walter has reached that point in life where he is having to face the realities of unfulfilled dreams. If he lives long enough there comes a time in the life of every man when he must realize that he will not attain certain goals he has set for himself. The majority of his years are behind him. It is very easy for Walter as well as other persons around this age to develop a complex in which he is always looking backward with despair rather than looking forward with hope. When this happens, like Lot's wife, a person turns into "a pillar of salt."

Walter's second problem is what I call an "Elijah complex." Faced with several problems, Walter is very much like Elijah who sat down under a juniper tree thinking that he was the only one of God's people. Actually, he is pitying himself, which may be an enjoyable activity for some people but adds very little in the way of positive help in overcoming one's problems.

Third, and perhaps foremost, is the "Willie Loman complex." Arthur Miller in *The Death of a Salesman* tells of Willie Loman, who always envisioned himself to be a type of super-salesman. Willie actually did not have the ability that he thought he possessed. One day, Willie had to face the reality of his ability. Unable to accept this reality, Willie was driven to alcohol. Finally, Willie died at a premature age. Two people stood by Willie's grave. One commented to another, "He never really knew who he was." This may be Walter's problem. He may have had visions of unrealistic worlds to be conquered.

Walter's disappointment and despair has affected his relationships with other persons. I note that he does not get along very well with his sons. Certainly he's had difficulty relating to the younger executives coming into the company. And, I wonder if perhaps his relationship with his wife is not due to her inequitable love and understanding. I have a feeling that she is very long on patience and endurance.

How can we help Walter? First, I think he must be faced with some realities. It would perhaps be too shocking to bring up all at once the problems I have mentioned here. However, Walter needs to be led to set, for himself, some realistic goals. Having felt that he has failed in so many respects, Walter needs one good solid success to start him on the route toward confidence in himself.

Also, I get the distinct impression that while Walter has busied himself with the daily routines of his job, he has ignored his emotional and spiritual needs. The helping hand of the Christian community could give Walter the friends that he so vitally needs at this point. Get him to attend a Sunday School class. Ask one or two Christian businessmen to show an interest in Walter. Help him to realize that he can find an identity in who he is rather than what he does.

"He Definitely Has a Mind of His Own"

Norman L. Bowman

Janet Stevens curled up in the big armchair by the window and began to write a letter to her sister.

> Dear Elizabeth:
> It's strange how little we really understand until we experience something firsthand.

Then she paused to reflect on what she had written. Three years before when her oldest son, John, enrolled in the state university, Elizabeth had sent two items. "A present for the parents of the graduate," she had said. One was a contemporary card offering "congratulations and condolences." The other was a paperback copy of a novel—*You Can't Go Home Again* by Thomas Wolfe. Janet had at first thought the gift was a little strange, but then she got the point. Her little boy was leaving home, and he could never really come back again. At the time, she and her husband had shrugged off the possibility with one of those "it will never happen to us" attitudes. But my, how right Elizabeth had been. Three years had made a great difference in John. He wasn't a little boy anymore. He definitely had a mind of his own. And the events of recent months had caused them some serious worry.

John was a bright young man. He had always been a good

student, was well behaved, and was genuinely interested in other people. Church activities had been a major emphasis in the Stevens' home and John had always participated enthusiastically. It was at this point that Janet and her husband were most concerned. During the past three years John had grown increasingly skeptical about religion. He rarely went to church, and when he did he was highly critical of the sermon and of the people who attended. He was pleasant enough about other subjects, but when friends or family talked of religion he was irritable and often sarcastic. It just didn't seem like John—at least not like the trusting, easy going John who had been so active in the church during high school. In fact, during a recent weekend at home, John had an argument with his parents and angrily told his mother that he didn't believe in God anymore and that he thought the church was just a refuge for hypocrites and hypochondriacs who loved to delude themselves.

Janet continued her letter to Elizabeth and confessed how the three-year-old warning had come home to roost. John had left home, and although he returned often enough for a visit, he was a much different person in many ways than they had ever known before. It seemed he had rejected the faith they had spent their lives trying to instil in him. This thought left them feeling hurt and very much alone.

Writing the letter helped to clarify her thinking, and Janet determined that she had to do something to resolve this family turmoil. She and her husband had been unable to talk with John about his attitudes so perhaps she could find a more neutral person who could.

On Janet's request, George Parker made a point to see John. George was a young deacon in the church and had been John's Sunday School teacher several years before. He traveled on business and frequently visited the university. He and John had dinner and then went to John's apartment for the rest of the evening to talk.

George had expected John to be noncommittal or perhaps a little bit hostile. But on the contrary, he was quite open and frank about his attitudes and seemed genuinely happy that George had come by, even if it was at his mother's request. He recounted the episode when he had told his mother he no longer believed in God.

"I don't guess I really meant that, and I'm sorry I shook Mom up," John said. "It was just that I was fed up and angry with the same old unthinking ritual of home-town churchianity. I suppose I do still believe in God. But I certainly don't accept the fairy tales I grew up on, about Jesus being some kind of super-cool junior deity. Jesus was a great teacher and a charismatic leader, but the rest of that divinity stuff is all a folk legend."

George, a bit surprised by John's candor and by his fervor, replied, "You puzzle me. How come you're so sure that these teachings you grew up on are just fairy tales?"

"I'm no biblical scholar, but I have done enough independent study to know that what the New Testament says about Christ isn't consistent from one book to the next. Granted, most of the accounts of Jesus' life have a historical basis, but when the stories about him were passed by word of mouth for a generation or two they got embellished all out of proportion. It's the same thing that happened with John Bunyan or Pecos Bill in American folklore. If people want to believe something remarkable badly enough, then pretty soon they begin confusing their fantasies with fact."

"Then you are convinced the Bible is riddled through with

man's fantasy and can't be relied upon as the Word of God?"
asked George.

"What is the Word of God? I'm not sure I understand that
kind of talk, even though I've heard it all my life. Does God
really speak? I've never heard his voice, and I don't know
anyone who has."

John paused for a moment, lit a cigarette, and blew the
smoke in a slow deliberate stream through the circle of light
below the table lamp. "It seems every time I go to Sunday
School the lesson is on Adam and Eve in the Garden of Eden
and how God created all the animals and the trees and put
them there all at once for Adam to take care of. People call
that the Word of God and say that if you don't believe it
happened just that way then you are some kind of heretical
atheist. Last year I took a course in biology and geology
during the same semester. In two weeks' time I reviewed
enough laboratory evidence of evolutionary processes to shoot
the first three chapters of Genesis all to pieces. People can get
all up tight over whether Adam had a navel. To me it doesn't
matter. I think it's pretty clear that probably the first thirteen
chapters of Genesis are mythological stories developed by
generations of men to explain the unexplainable. They are
good stories, but I don't think we can justify them by calling
them the Word of God.

As George listened, he hoped his face was not revealing
what was in his mind. He disagreed strongly with what John
had said, both about the New Testament account of Jesus' life
and about the accuracy of the Genesis creation story. But at
this point, he didn't want to make an issue with John over the
question of biblical revelation.

"It seems to me," he ventured, "that the accuracy of the

Bible has to be weighed in terms of the role it has played in the lives of men. A lot of good men have accepted it as truth and followed its moral teachings. For a book which you say is undependable, it certainly has stood the test of centuries."

"I'm not questioning the value of the Bible," retorted John. "The Bible contains a great deal of truth and beauty. I just object to the way people practice a self-delusion and call their delusion faith. Take the average pious church member. He doesn't know anything about what the Bible really says, because he has never read it critically. He thinks biblical criticism is a communist plot. Faith to that kind of person is an unthinking blind trust. He equates honest intellectual doubt with blasphemy against God."

George was slowly stirring a freshly poured cup of coffee. He took a moment before answering and squashed several of the tiny bubbles against the rim of his spoon. "Aren't you overstating that a little, John? I don't know many people who really think like that."

"Maybe they don't verbalize their feelings, but I think the mentality is there just the same. Have you ever seen the little chicken at the amusement park, where you put in the quarter and the hen dances or plunks the toy piano to get her food? Church people are a lot like that. The fact that they behave a certain way isn't because they have thought the issues through or have legitimate reasons to react the way they do. They are just like the chicken who has been conditioned to act in a prescribed manner."

George looked puzzled. "I'm not sure I follow you."

"Psychologists have done a great deal of work in analyzing human behavior and finding ways to modify that behavior. The chicken I just mentioned is one of the classic experiments to show how animals can be trained to behave in any way, through a system of rewarding desired behavior and punishing undesired behavior. People are no different. We just have a more complex conditioning program called society. We are shaped by our environment. Acceptable behavior is rewarded with respectability. Unacceptable behavior is either punished or is rewarded by ostracism. Pretty soon we are dancing just like the chicken. We dress alike; we act alike; we mouth the same opinions; we blindly accept the same conclusions because that is the rewarding thing to do in our society. Being religious is respectable and profitable. I don't hold this against people. If they want to delude themselves, that's their business. I just don't want them to expect me to accept their self-delusions as some kind of divinely inspired universal moral law."

George, much to his own consternation, didn't have an answer. He didn't agree with John, but then he didn't disagree with him entirely either. He wondered how John felt about his own Christian conversion experience when he was a Junior boy. "You don't sound like you have much faith in God's ability to work in a person's life. John, I remember very clearly when you made a profession of faith when you were about twelve. Wasn't that experience a real and meaningful one to you?"

John heard the question but he didn't answer for quite a while. He sat there quietly with his feet on the coffee table. He blew a lone smoke ring that drifted lazily beneath the lampshade and seemed to hang forever in the warm still air. "Mom and Dad mean a lot to me," he replied, "and I wouldn't want to do anything that would hurt them. But the trouble is, we just don't see things from the same world view."

"How's that, John?"

"Well, everything is simple for them—it's either black or

white, good or bad, pro or con. Mom told me once that the night I walked down the aisle and made my profession of faith she felt a great burden lift from her shoulders. She felt relieved knowing that I was saved. Well, I thought about that for a long time. I hadn't felt a burden lift from my shoulders, and I thought that something must be wrong. Conversion just wasn't what Mom and Dad had made it seem. The church was so much a part of my life that I didn't have any kind of emotional experience or dramatic change in life style. I just responded in the way everyone expected me to."

"You mean you joined the church because of the pressure of what people expected of you?" George asked.

"Well, I wouldn't call it pressure. I think it was a normal reaction under the circumstances. I think everyone is controlled more or less by the environmental situation they live in or by the basic elements of personality which are inbred. I was a very trusting, accepting, and obedient boy, and I responded in a pattern consistent with those characteristics. It may have been a real experience then, but as the Bible says, on becoming a man I have put away those childish things."

"Are you concerned with your salvation, John? I know your parents have been quite worried over your apparent rejection of the Christian faith."

"You see! That's what I mean by different world views. Mom and Dad get all up tight over whether I'm saved. Their minds ask the simple questions: Is he or isn't he? But those questions never really occur to me. I don't think it makes one bit of difference to God whether I utter some mumbo jumbo about belief or whether I subscribe to some church covenant. If there is a God and he is really God then he must know the real me. I shouldn't have to conform to someone else's standard in order for God to understand me. It seems that we have little control over our lives and the existential situation we find ourselves in is going to dominate everything we do. I may live in affluence and the next man live in squalor. If this is the case, we can't expect to operate on the same value system and relate to God through the same official channels. And what's more, we can't do much to change our environment. So I think the most important thing to do is to face what life brings us with courage and to live out our lives day by day with integrity. I'm not happy over all the doubts and questions I have in my mind. And I haven't set out deliberately to part ways with the faith of the family. But I am sure of one thing—my doubts are honest and I have nothing to apologize for.

It was nearly midnight, and both George and John were weary from a long day. They hadn't really settled anything, but they had cleared the air. Both had enjoyed the visit and had the warm feeling of an accepting relationship. They would meet again soon and try to go beyond the meeting of hearts to a meeting of minds.

————◆———

Analysis by WALTER C. JACKSON

Every young man moves from dependence on parents to seek his own level of independence as an adult. John had spent the most formative years of independence away from home and the environment of his childhood. His world view had broadened, and he had begun to define himself in terms other than those of his parents.

John's first need was for a genuine companionship. In George he found an understanding friend who accepted him in spite of what he believed intellectually. Anyone who will help a theological doubter needs this quality of relationship. George was open, concerned, yet honestly representative of his own basic faith. Also, George did not permit their conversations to degenerate into a religious argument. This would have been a serious error. What John needed was some examples of Christians like George; people he knows who really do behave as if they had faith in a loving, forgiving Lord.

A second need for John is to become acquainted with some of the intellectual giants of Christian faith whose strength is in the area of honest scholarship and not simply in the techniques of overpowering doubters. The critical study of the Bible has been taught in Baptist seminaries since before the turn of this century. An alert pastor will be able to introduce John to the positive results of those students and to offer some illuminating reading materials. Baptist apologists like Eric C. Rust have shown that the discoveries of science are not inconsistent with Christian faith. To let John think that no man of faith has worked through form criticism and evolution and still remained a Christian is an injustice. It would be an injustice to him and to the men of faith whose lives bear testimony to the truth that God is alive and that faith in him is both emotionally and intellectually possible.

A third need John has is to discover that there are Christians who are thoroughly trained in the behavioral sciences. They, too, understand that many obedient children trust the adult world and its patterns of religion enough to commit themselves in faith. They also know that children grow into mature adulthood and affirm the life of faith in God with emotional and intellectual competence. Such a person is not in eternal revolt against his childhood experiences. In fact, he is able to embrace the positive childhood experiences and extend their meaning in the existential here and now of his adult world. Relevant adult life requires a strength of character which is enhanced by, and not reduced by, Christian faith.

Mrs. Stephens, her family, and perhaps the entire church fellowship of John's childhood may need some attention. Through John and George, they will have the opportunity to work through some of the intellectual challenges to the Christian faith presented by the twentieth century. They will have opportunity to grow with John and may give him an opportunity to share his newly strengthened faith, if and when he achieves it.

If he becomes frozen in his state of doubt and agnosticism toward Christianity, the church may become motivated to provide competent instruction for young people in their middle teens to anchor their lives through faith in Christ. No young Christian active in a church in the twentieth century should be deprived of the opportunity of studying his faith in light of the real and true discoveries scientists have made about God's universe.

In any event, a proper Christian posture toward John is openness and love. Thank God he definitely has a mind of his own.

———————◆———————

Analysis by JAMES M. ROBINSON

In thinking of how to minister in this case, the first inclination is to rush to the aid of John Stevens. John does need help, and there is a real opportunity here for ministry. However, the need of his father and mother must not be overlooked. A ministry to them must also be established.

Janet Stevens and her husband need a pastoral visit. Since they consider their son's problem to be spiritual, they need to talk it over with their spiritual advisor. Their pastor can help them to see that some intellectual doubt is inevitable as the child matures into an adult. When a person becomes a Christian as a child, his understanding of the Christian experience is on a childish level. He believes what he knows about the Bible and Christianity because of what someone else has told him. If he ever becomes an effective Christian, he must come to believe what he believes on the basis of his own examination and experience. As he makes the transition from secondhand to personal belief, doubt is inevitable. John's parents need to see, as apparently John himself already does, that honest doubt is no cause for shame. They need to understand that most youngsters rebel to some degree as they grow older and that ordinarily they make their rebellious attitude appear deeper and more serious than it actually is.

In the attempt to minister to John, George Parker seems to be the key. He is off to a good start. His relationship with John seems to be excellent. He did not try to solve any of John's problems immediately. He did not offer himself as an expert on the Bible or theology. He did not register shock at John's attitudes or beliefs. He left the door open for further discussion. A trained counselor could not have done better.

Since John's pastor is also George's pastor, George might enlist the pastor's help. The pastor could offer George some help on the knotty problems of form criticism, evolution, and existentialism. He might suggest some resource material on these subjects which George could read. Although George needs some knowledge in these areas, it would not be wise for him to attempt to solve all of John's problems at once. The central issue is John's attitude toward and relationship with

Christ. He should be encouraged to find out all he can about Christ both from biblical and secular sources. Gradually, the question ought to be raised as to whether Christ could be a genuinely good and wise man if he were not actually what he claimed to be—the Son of God.

John's doubts must be dealt with honestly and seriously. He, too, should be led to see that such doubts are normal for the intelligent young person and that God is not offended by these. Some attempt must be made to separate in John's mind weak Christians from unreliable Christianity. A Christian who fails must not be equated with the failure of Christianity. John has confused Christians who do not work their religion with a religion that will not work. He should be encouraged to try Christianity as the Bible sets it forth rather than as he sees it practiced.

A letter from John's pastor would be beneficial, not as an attempt to enter into the dialogue but as a way of expressing the interest of John's church in him. The pastor may or may not reveal his awareness of John's doubts. At any rate, he should let George continue what he has already begun rather than trying to work with John himself.

This case may well point out two churches that are also in need of ministry—John's home church and his college church. One did not prepare him for what he would face at college and the other is not communicating with him. One has needs in the area of prevention and the other in the area of cure.

John has a problem, and he needs to be ministered unto. Yet, there are problems which are satelite to his, and these must not be neglected.

---◄◆►---

Analysis by JOHN ISHEE

I see in this case study three persons experiencing stress and anxiety in different degrees. First, John's mother is anxious about his new ideas. She loves him, or she would not be concerned for his welfare. Second, George, the deacon, is anxious because he is not quite sure how to relate to John or how to answer his questions. Finally, John is anxious because he is living with a troubled mind. His rapid exposure to new ideas in college has not allowed him time to assimilate them into his storehouse of experience. I see him as a concerned but honest young man.

John's concern seems to focus around four false assumptions. His greatest need is for someone to help him explore these assumptions and arrive at valid conclusions. The first assumption is that a person cannot take a critical look at the Bible. While it is true that the Bible is a book of faith, scholars have looked at it in a critical manner and thus have provided us a more rational basis for our faith. John needs to be put in touch with some sources that will help him reconcile the inconsistencies he feels at this point.

Second, there is an assumption that the theory of evolution is totally inconsistent with the Bible. Personally, I do not believe this is so. However, John may have some difficulty finding answers to this false assumption within the context of his local church. Unfortunately, when many people think about evolution they consider only the idea that man descended from a monkey. Evolution is far broader than this and has far more implications. For too long, church leaders have chosen to ignore the theory of evolution with the hope that it would go away. However, all facts point to the indication that it is not going away. John needs to be encouraged to continue his search for answers in this area. The concept of evolution is not all bad. Many lives have been saved in hospitals as a result of Darwin's discovery of the consistencies between lower animal life and the life of a human being.

The third assumption is that behaviorism has all the answers. Probably John has studied about Watson's behaviorism which has experienced renewal under the leadership of B. F. Skinner. Behaviorism is making a worthwhile contribution in the lives of many people today. For example, in the mental retardation laboratory at George Peabody College in Nashville, Tennessee, mentally retarded and emotionally disturbed children are often taught basic skills which help them to function better in life. However, for the person of the average intelligence, the idea of being shaped entirely by the environment is not the entire story. Man filters his external environment through his own perceptions and cognitions. John evidently has had a considerable amount of study in psychology. However, I suggest that he continue his psychological studies by reading some of the works of Carl Rogers and other phenomenological or perceptional psychologists.

Finally, John's last assumption is that the church must, of necessity, be out-of-date. This is not true. While the church is often slow in moving into new approaches in its ministry, many creative and exciting things are happening today in the church. The entire church renewal movement is seeking to discover a new relevance for the church in modern society. John needs to become a fellow pilgrim in discovering new ways a church can be made relevant to the needs of people. And, he needs also to be reminded that many needs of people are being met within the structures of the church today.

There is an admirable honesty about John. In my efforts to help him, I would ask him to state four or five basic questions that give him the most trouble in his faith. Then, I would go on a pilgrimage with John in seeking to discover the answers to these questions. Who knows—in the process I might even learn something myself!

"My Youngster Is Taking Drugs!"

Jean Potts

"But there must be some mistake," she said when they called and told her why Raymond wasn't home from school. "No! I don't believe it!"

And when she repeated the message to George—who had come in just as she was hanging up—he had been as incredulous as she.

Their son caught using drugs? Impossible! It happened— they knew that, of course. But to other kids—juvenile delinquents, misfits, the underprivileged, the neglected, the unloved. Not to a bright wholesome boy like Raymond, who had always done so well at school, in sports and music; who went to church and Sunday school regularly; who had a home he could bring his friends to, parents he could depend on.

She still had moments—like that first one, six months ago— of dazed disbelief. It couldn't have happened; it was all a crazy nightmare. She would wake up in the morning and find herself and George and Raymond safe and sound, back in their own stable world.

Stable? She had thought so, until without warning it had shattered around her ears. Raymond under arrest; he and his best friend, Ken, picked up with narcotics in their possession. "Bombed," both of them. (It had been just a word before;

now it was carved into her brain, along with the rest of the ugly vocabulary—skag, and grass, and acid; on a trip; sucking a cube.) Raymond, sullen and remote, brought up before the juvenile court and, after almost a week under lock and key, released into his parents' custody on probation. Front-page news, with only the boys' names withheld because of their age. Ken was a little younger, not quite 15. They were expelled from school. During the quarter Raymond's grades, except in music, had been all F's. What else, when he had skipped classes half the time?

And neither she nor George had known! The cut classes, the forged excuses, the lies about why he needed extra money— those were things other kids did. Not Raymond. They had gone along, blind to any change in him, completely unaware of the rank underground world he was living in.

Ken's parents had not known either. No doubt their outbursts, once they got Ken home, followed much the same pattern as their own—from upbraiding to reproach to anguished pleading to frantic warning. And did Ken lash back at his parents in scorn and defiance, as Raymond had done one night? "You've never tried it," he'd said. "How do you know it's so terrible?"

Afterward George had tried to brush it off: "Just his way of shutting us up. I guess we were laying it on pretty heavy." But she knew that those words of Raymond's haunted him as much as they did her. Since then she had come to recognize a particular expression on George's face—a sort of tremor of shock and dread that struck out of the blue—sometimes just when the three of them most seemed as they used to be.

Now, for example. They sat at the dinner table; Raymond, having polished off his second piece of chocolate pie, was saying, with a smile of candid boyish pleasure, "Not bad, Mom."

And even as he smiled back, the tremor crossed George's face. She, too, saw it and remembered.

But there was nothing to worry about, really. Raymond was making better-than-average grades in the new school they had managed to get him into. The six months' probation was almost over, with no marks against him to prevent his being legally cleared. Surely they could trust their son not to slip back into that poisonous underground world.

"Better get going, you two," she said as she started clearing the table. "You don't have too much time."

One of the interests they shared was woodworking. For the past few months they had been attending weekly classes together at the "Y." Raymond himself had suggested it—further proof that there was no cause for worry.

On her way to the kitchen she glanced back at them. George was on his feet, but Raymond was still sitting there. Eyes lowered. Face closed up. Her heart sank. "You go ahead, Dad," he mumbled to the tablecloth. "Not me."

"What do you mean, not you?"

"Aw, it's no fun without a workroom of our own."

"What kind of excuse is that?" George began angrily. "There's no space for a workroom in an apartment this size, even if we could afford the equipment. Nobody else in the class has a workroom of his own. So what's all this? Last week it was great stuff, and now all at once . . ."

Now all at once it was gone—the hope they had clung to, the comforting assurance that for a few hours, at least, Raymond would be kept busy and happy and safe. In its place, nothing —emptiness, a terrifying dangerous gap.

"Okay," George said at last. "So we don't go to class. You got any other plans for tonight?"

Raymond hunched his shoulders. His eyes remained fixed on the tablecloth. "Nothing special. Some of the guys are coming over later."

It seemed to her that George aged before her eyes. He stood for a moment, gray and beaten, staring at his son's bent head. Then he turned and went into the living room.

She joined him there when the dishes were done. "Some of the guys" turned out to be, as usual, Ken and two other boys who had dropped out of their home schools and were now attending the one that had accepted Raymond. That they were still best friends was only natural. Just as it was only natural that the dropouts—all with the same dubious background—should gravitate toward one another.

She sat on the sofa, pretending to sew; George was in the big chair, pretending to read. Their eyes kept straying to the closed door of Raymond's room. The four boys were playing records in there. Now and then below the beat of the music, she caught the sound of low-pitched conversation, a muffled laugh. ("You've never tried it. How do you know it's so terrible?") Near-panic gripped her; she was on the verge of flying apart when George suddenly surged out of his chair and began pacing the floor.

"Don't," she said. "It's all right—it's going to be all right." He stopped in front of her, and she went on, in a chattering whisper: "We mustn't worry like this. We'll think of something else, a new interest for him. We have to trust him, George. Just because it happened before, that doesn't mean . . . We have to trust him!"

"Yes." Then, in a voice rough with suffering, he asked, "But how can we? How can we?"

This case study was reprinted from *Family Circle*, October, 1969. A Fawcett Publication. Used by permission.

------◄◆►------

Analysis by WALTER C. JACKSON

This brief description of the relationship between Raymond and his parents suggests a problem of rather large proportions. Both child and parents talk at each other rather than *to* or *with* each other. Raymond's parents take great pride in his conforming behavior and react vindictively toward any indication that Raymond just might have some independent plans of his own.

While this may be stretching a point with such a brief account of their relationship, it is reinforced by the manner in which Raymond's free time is shepherded by his parents. Raymond's move to become involved in a woodworking class with his father sounds like appeasement rather than genuine creative interest. The reluctance of the parents to give some trust to Raymond after he had begun the drug habit is understandable, but there appears to have been no constructive attempt to open lines of communication for the reestablishment of that trust.

An apparently unreal dimension of this story has to do with the expulsion of the boys from school after the court released them on probation—especially for first offenders. This is more punitive than a twentieth century school, especially a public one, should be. Indeed, it may be illegal. In a normal setting, the parents, the court through its probation officer assigned to the boys, and the school counselor could make a team covenant concerning the rehabilitation plan. The boys would return to a familiar setting and be required to work through their probation with maximum responsibility.

The local pastor and knowledgeable adults in the church whose activities touch Raymond and Ken in any way could also be counted upon for supportive help. Especially, the pastor can give attention to the family dimension of the problem, begin supportive and insightful counseling, and be the person who, in consultation with the school counselor, may make a decision to recommend additional professional help. The selection would depend on the circumstances, but possibly consultation with an area child guidance clinic or with a regional comprehensive care center may be indicated.

Hopefully, Raymond's parents will be led to an awareness of their own responsibility in this matter and begin some realistic changes in their attitudes and behavior toward Raymond. Focusing on Raymond's strength in music might provide a key if some form of creative outlet for this talent can be found. The best goal is to try to preserve Raymond's integrity as a person: that is, his right to independence as well as his need to recognize the realistic boundaries set by his parents.

Few problems are worthy of such open social action as the current drug traffic. Friends who are able by talent and desire could mount a citizens' campaign in cooperation with local school and civil authorities against the traffic in drugs. Police departments across the country are usually understaffed in the narcotics division. A campaign to employ additional personnel, suitably equipped, may serve a twofold purpose. It may limit the drug traffic and possibly save some of Raymond's friends and younger classmates from the same temptations which proved to be Raymond's downfall. A second campaign to secure a more enlightened school administration in a situation as the one described is also indicated. This would insure a climate more conducive to rehabilitation.

――――――◆◆――――――

Analysis by JAMES M. ROBINSON

Raymond's parents are despondent and feel that they have failed in the attempt to raise their son properly. They feel guilty and all alone. They need some help. Both of them need someone who will simply convey the message that other people still care about them. They need someone who can help them understand what has happened to them and to their son.

Obviously, Raymond's mother and father need more information on narcotics. They apparently do not have any knowledge concerning the reasons for narcotic experimentation nor are they able to explain to their son why the use of narcotics can be condemned without having been tried. It would be well if a respected Christian friend could point out to them that simply because a boy experiments with narcotics does not mean that he no longer can be trusted in any area. Of course, no one would make light of narcotic experimentation. The person who feels the need for such experimentation has a problem of some kind that is not a normal problem. Some lack exists in his life, and the nature and reason for this lack must be identified. Still, a person is not to be considered useless just because he has tried narcotics.

Raymond's mother and father must be led to see his need for an attitude of trust on the part of his parents. Although they must not attempt to minimize the seriousness of his actions, they must be willing to admit that they, too, bear part of the guilt. To see his hesitancy to continue the class at the YMCA as an excuse to return to former actions is unfair. His statement that woodworking held little interest for him as long as there was no possibility of doing any of it except at the class is reasonable. If such statements were taken at face value, the relationship between Ray and his parents would be better. Too, Raymond's failure to handle freedom in the past does not mean that all freedom must now be withdrawn. He was given more freedom at first than he could handle. This does not mean, however, that he is incapable of handling any freedom at all.

Raymond needs help from his parents and from interested Christian friends. He, too, feels a sense of guilt, failure, and isolation. By staying away from him, others can add to this feeling. He needs some new friends and would likely be open to new friendships if he felt they were offered out of genuine care and concern. If no new friendships are offered, this will automatically send him back to his old circle of friends. This would be a prime time for some of the young people at the church to offer a warm invitation to Raymond to participate in some of the youth activities. Also, some of the adult workers with young people could make a special effort to let Raymond know that they have not written him off because of his mistakes.

Something must be found to capture Raymond's interest and to give him a sense of accomplishment and success. The clue to what this might be can be found in the fact that even while Raymond was failing other subjects, he was doing well in music. This interest in and talent for music should certainly be encouraged. Every effort should be made to find an area in which Raymond might become enthusiastically involved. No reasonable expense should be considered too great.

The prognosis in Raymond's case is encouraging. He has given his parents no trouble during the six month probation period. With Christian help and support, this crisis situation can be met successfully.

Analysis by JOHN ISHEE

These parents have a real problem. I feel inadequate to comment because I have had so little experience with persons taking drugs. And, I might add, I pray that as a parent I will never have experience of this nature. I am tempted to offer sympathy to the parents. They need it. However, mere sympathy would be of very little help to them in overcoming their problems.

First, I must commend the parents for seeking to establish a more wholesome relationship with their son. I get the very distinct impression that they are really trying to relate to their son in a positive way. I commend them for it.

Second, I get the impression that the life style of the child is being set more by his peers than by his parents. This is not unusual, especially for a person who is Raymond's age. During adolescence, acceptance by the group is of primary importance. Much of the reinforcement for behavior, whether good or bad, comes from those with whom the adolescent associates. Therefore, I would give serious attention to helping Raymond establish more wholesome relationships with other adolescents. It is not unusual that he should gravitate toward those persons who have similar experiences. However, while this is not unusual, neither is it always the best. The parents are correct in seeing the need to trust Raymond, but trust is always a matter of degree and never an absolute. Raymond needs to be trusted as much as possible, but he also needs some very positive guidance to help him avoid a pitfall that could ruin his life. The most loving thing the parents could do is to prohibit Raymond from associating with friends that may encourage his use of drugs. This is especially true in light of his history of using drugs in the past.

Third, Raymond's parents—as well as most other parents— need to improve their knowledge of drugs. By knowing more about this problem, they will be better equipped to face the issue with their children and engage in prevention of the use of drugs rather than helping a child to overcome the use of drugs after he is addicted to them. The Christian Life Commission has an excellent pamphlet on drugs which is available for a nominal charge. In addition, a new book, *How to Fight the Drug Menace* is available. (See Resources.) I suggest that the parents become more knowledgeable of drugs and what they can do to prevent their use.

"I Am a Little Devil"

Ray Cooley

It was Sunday morning worship at Woodlawn Baptist Church, and the congregation was singing the hymn of invitation. A frail eighteen-year-old girl slipped from the pew where she had been sitting. Slowly she advanced to the front of the church, then knelt at a railing which separated the pews from the platform.

Although the congregation began singing the final stanza of the hymn, Dorothy continued to kneel and pray. So Reverend Walters, the minister, invited her to stand. Dorothy rose to her feet slowly. Her body was rigid and her hands trembling. The minister asked Dorothy the reason for her response to the invitation. The girl replied, just above a mumble, "I want to be saved." But her posture and expression betrayed a hopeless feeling. It seemed that she doubted that God could ever forgive her.

Reverend Walters was perplexed. Dorothy had been baptized at age twelve in Woodlawn Church. She came to church regularly with her mother and a sister and was known in the church as a particularly serious and dedicated young person. Two years ago she announced to the church that God had called her into full-time Christian service. Dorothy was shy, yet she was willing to do anything she could to prepare herself to be "a workman who has no need to be ashamed" (2 Tim. 2:15, RSV). But in recent months, she had seemed less sure of herself. Now she seemed despondent and was asking to be saved.

Reverend Walters asked Dorothy to remain after the service so that he could have a few words with her. He announced to the congregation that Dorothy Scott was anxious to serve the Lord and that he would be talking with her about it. The minister knew that many members of the congregation were also perplexed about Dorothy's behavior, and perhaps he wanted to reassure them that he would be helping Dorothy.

When most of the people had left the church, and the few left were in the back talking, Reverend Walters invited Dorothy to sit down in the front pew with him. He began, "Dorothy, you feel that you aren't saved?"

She was quiet, tense, unable even to look her pastor in the eye. Finally she said, with considerable difficulty, "I know that I'm guilty. The Lord is telling me to be saved. I *want* to be saved. But I hope that I haven't crossed the invisible line. Maybe my heart is so hardened that God cannot save me. I feel so *evil*."

Reverend Walters wondered why Dorothy felt so guilty. Had she done something that she was very ashamed of? "God forgives us all our sins," he tried to reassure Dorothy. "You have been a loyal church member; you've worked hard for the Lord. It is difficult for me to believe that God has turned away from you." He waited for a response. Dorothy winced as if she felt even stronger the pain of condemnation.

The minister then invited Dorothy to pray with him. She insisted that they get down on their knees, because she "needed to humble herself." Reverend Walters obliged quietly. Hesitantly, tearfully, repetitiously, Dorothy prayed that

God would save her. Then her pastor thanked God for his love so grandly demonstrated in Christ's sacrifice and asked God to guide his servant Dorothy. After the prayer there were several minutes of silence. It seemed forever. Finally, Dorothy rose slowly to her feet and uttered a meek, "Thank you," then turned and walked slowly away. Her pastor obviously felt helpless as he watched her leave.

Dorothy's mother was waiting outside the church where she was visiting with friends. One of the friends had just finished commenting, "Dorothy is such a fine girl, so anxious to do what is right."

"Yes," Mrs. Scott replied, "but sometimes we wonder if she isn't too religious."

"Here she comes now," said the friend, as Dorothy slowly descended the church's front steps.

Dorothy seemed embarrassed by her mother's friends, who were all watching as she reached the sidewalk. "Come on, Dorothy, it's getting late! We must hurry home to get dinner for your dad. You know how he is when dinner isn't ready on time!" The Scott family hurried to their car and drove away.

Mr. Scott was annoyed that his wife and children were late coming home. He had stopped going to church several years back when he had a falling out with several members of the Woodlawn Church. He promised never again to worry himself with those "hypocrites." "What on earth kept you so long?" he demanded.

"Oh, Dorothy went down front this morning," Mrs. Scott answered. Dorothy, who was in the next room, overheard the conversation and was even more embarrassed. "It concerns me," Mrs. Scott continued, "you know how she has been lately."

"Oh my gosh," her husband replied, "I told you that little

devil is too religious. All that she thinks about is how bad she is. Huh! She ought to get acquainted with some of my friends at the plant. She'd know what life is all about." "Dorothy! Dorothy! Come here!" called Mr. Scott.

"Yes, Dad," Dorothy answered quietly but with obvious annoyance.

"Honey, I just don't understand you. Why do you feel so guilty? Been out with a boy?" He knew well that Dorothy never dated. In fact, this was a bone of contention between them. Dorothy blushed as her father continued, "Dorothy, you're eighteen. Isn't it time that you stopped worrying so much about your religion and gave more attention to what you are going to do in life? You can't live in this house forever, you know." Mr. Scott turned to his wife and snapped, "Come on, woman, you know how hungry I am. Get that food on the table!"

Dorothy left the room, thinking to herself, "Dad called me a little devil. That's exactly what I am, a little d-e-v-i-l!"

Dorothy had finished high school in June. Now it was November, and she had no plans for a job, marriage, or further education. She helped her mother around the house some, but with little zest for life. In recent months she had spent more and more time to herself.

Sunday afternoon was Mrs. Scott's favorite time. She was fond of playing the old gospel tunes on the piano. Sometimes the children would sing along, although usually she played and sang by herself. She was a good pianist and playing helped her to get away from it all. Dorothy enjoyed listening to her mother play. "Mom is such a good Christian," she would tell herself. Mrs. Scott went to church every time the doors were open. She insisted on family Bible readings, though Dad usually left the room when she read. And Mom made sure that grace was said at meals and that the children said their prayers each night.

"Mom has such a hard time with me," Dorothy thought to herself. "I can't do a thing right! All I am is a burden to her."

Just yesterday while Dorothy was trying to iron some clothes for the family, Mrs. Scott had grabbed the iron from her shouting, "Dorothy, you're too slow! Child, when are you going to learn that a woman has to work hard to keep a family going? You may have a family someday, you know . . . if anybody will have you. Oh! You're so lazy. Let me finish that ironing. You make more work than you are a help."

Dorothy's mother was impatient. "But why not?" mused Dorothy. "After all, when you have a dummy like me for a daughter, you're bound to be impatient."

Dorothy left the house that Sunday afternoon because she felt too guilty to stay in her mother's presence. She retreated to the garage and dropped to her knees to pray. She remained on her knees on cold, bare concrete for almost an hour. When her father discovered her there, he was angry. "God would love you more if you helped your mother the way you should instead of spending so much time in prayer," he lectured.

Louise was Dorothy's younger sister. She was only one year younger than Dorothy and they were good companions. In recent months, as Dorothy withdrew to herself, Louise first got angry, then disgusted. But as time passed and Louise began to sense that something really was wrong with Dorothy, something Dorothy was unable to cope with, Louise felt guilty for the unkind things that she had said to and about her sister. Louise had looked up to Dorothy and respected her as a dedicated Christian with high morals, but more recently she wondered if her older sister were going off the deep end in religion. She also feared that Dorothy might be sick, although neither of her parents seemed to consider that possibility. Louise wished that her mother and father could be more understanding.

Reverend Walters wondered what could be done to help Dorothy. He had an idea that her problem was not simply a spiritual one. Perhaps her depression and confusion were signs of illness. He decided to recommend that Dorothy see a doctor. So he telephoned Mrs. Scott.

Mrs. Scott was skeptical of the value of her pastor's recommendation. She knew that there was nothing physically wrong with Dorothy. But her daughter had continued to get worse, and she felt that something needed to be done. About ten days after the Sunday when Dorothy went to the front of the church, Mrs. Scott took her to their family physician.

The doctor recommended that Dorothy receive psychiatric treatment. The Scotts were shocked. They hadn't thought their daughter to be mentally ill. They knew that she was mixed up, but they had been hoping that she soon would snap out of her mood. The physician suggested that Dorothy might even make an attempt on her life, and so suggested that the Scotts consider hospitalizing their daughter for a short time. So, with mixed emotions, the Scott family faced the prospect of admitting Dorothy to a psychiatric hospital. They were unable to pay for private psychiatric care and decided to take her to a nearby state hospital. The doctor suggested that Dorothy would receive competent treatment there.

Mrs. Scott was afraid and embarrassed. She was fearful because, like most people, she had little awareness of what to expect in a state hospital. She wondered what kind of treatment Dorothy would receive. She was afraid that Dorothy might get worse in the hospital with all those "crazy folks." Mrs. Scott feared that her daughter might have to stay there for a long, indefinite time. She had heard a neighbor say, "Once you put a member of your family into Western State, you're putting her away for good." To top it off, of course, Mrs. Scott was not convinced that her daughter was that sick.

Mrs. Scott was embarrassed because she suspected that the neighbors and people at church would find plenty to talk about. They were apt to blame her for "putting her daughter away," or they might wonder if it weren't Mrs. Scott herself who needed the psychiatric care. Too, she was afraid the hospital staff might blame her and her husband for Dorothy's plight. Indeed, at a deeper level, Mrs. Scott feared that she could be at least in part responsible for her daughter's trouble.

Mr. Scott was angry and confused. "Why, if Dorothy would stop trying to be so religious, she'd be alright," he argued. He doubted that psychiatric treatment was the answer to Dorothy's problem. "What do those head shrinkers think they can do for Dorothy?" he asked. Mr. Scott was aware, too, that Dorothy's hospitalization was going to put an additional strain on the family budget. There would be even a modest charge for treatment at the state hospital, and hospitalization for psychiatric treatment was not covered by his medical insurance policy. The Scotts would have to pay the entire cost out of pocket, on top of the usual monthly bills.

Louise wondered what she would tell her friends at school. So many of them knew Dorothy as a good girl, although a little strange. "With a Mom and Dad like yours, it's no wonder Dorothy is sick," they might say, or at least think. As is true for most adolescents, what her friends thought was most important to Louise. Yet she would want to defend her parents. Louise also wondered if eventually she would become mentally ill, too. She had heard that mental illness runs in families.

Dorothy never resisted the idea of going to the hospital. Her feelings about it were difficult to sort. On the one hand, she felt that she deserved to be "put away." She failed to understand that her hospitalization was temporary and for treatment of her illness. After all, she didn't believe that she was sick, no matter what the doctor might have said. She felt that her real problem was her spiritual condition.

On the other hand Dorothy was afraid. She had heard rumors of the "electric treatment" that they use to treat patients at the state hospital. She had also heard the gossip that they had cells where they lock people up. Her fantasy of what the state hospital was like, a place of horror, was far from the decent treatment facility that it is. The doctor's assurance that she would receive good treatment did little to allay her apprehension.

After calling ahead to notify the hospital that they were bringing Dorothy for possible admission, Mr. and Mrs. Scott started out with their daughter. They were uncertain about this step into the unknown. Louise wanted to go along, but her mother insisted that she was too young to see the state hospital. This unnecessary rebuff made it more difficult for Louise.

Dorothy and her parents were relieved when they were received with kindness by the physician who interviewed Dorothy in the admissions area of the hospital. The pleasant attitude of the social worker who interviewed her parents set them at ease, too. The admitting physician agreed with the Scotts' family doctor that Dorothy could probably be treated with good results at the hospital. Since Dorothy was eighteen, the legal age of adulthood in her state, she was able to admit herself to the hospital voluntarily.

A nurse took Dorothy and her parents to the ward where

Dorothy would be staying. Though clean, the buildings were old and their hallways not well lighted. Seeing several patients who were confused intensified the Scotts' fears about leaving Dorothy at the hospital. But the nurse was helpful in explaining the hospital routine to Dorothy and her parents and that made them feel better again. So Mr. and Mrs. Scott left their daughter with mixed feelings. Hospital personnel had reinforced the Scotts' hopes that Dorothy would be well cared for, but they left still wondering if they had done the right thing for their daughter. They were anxious about their daughter's future, and how it would effect their own.

Analysis by WALTER C. JACKSON

Old wives' tales and rumors still give mental illness and its treatment a bad name in many places. Informed people, however, know that mental illness often responds to treatment as well as or better than physical illness, and that mental hospitals continually discharge rehabilitated patients back into active and productive community life. There should be no stigma attached to persons who seek and receive needed mental treatment.

Occasionally, signs of mental ill health will display themselves in the church. Dorothy's story is a tragic illustration of a child who has grown to the threshold of serious illness. Those wishing to minister to people like Dorothy will do well to remember a few of the signs of emotional instability which she displayed.

She was very shy and greatly depressed, spoke disparagingly of herself, was compulsive in religious ritual (kneeling for hours on cold concrete floors), and was unable to feel the liberating freedom from guilt in the normal exercise of her faith. Wanting to be "saved" over and over again is an inappropriate response to the gospel. Requests by one person for multiple rebaptisms is another such inappropriate response. Such acts may be recognized as "cries for help" from the person involved, signs that she is having so much trouble coping with her life situation that she is unable to enjoy the normal practice of her faith.

The fact that a regular worship service was the place where Dorothy's problems were brought to the surface should not go unnoticed. So much that is disguised as preaching is an assault on human emotions. It is disparaging, is guilt inducing and rarely mentions, if ever, the good news of acceptance, of forgiveness, of love. Where such preaching predominates, it is one of God's miracles that we do not see more young people with problems like Dorothy's.

The quality of Dorothy's home life is an additional indication of her need for help. Her low opinion of herself was confirmed by parents who told her they had a "dummy for a daughter," a child who was a "little devil." Friends close to this family could encourage them to talk about their part in Dorothy's illness without condemning them. They would also give support as the Scotts begin to do the kinds of things the family doctor and the psychiatrist at the state hospital encourage them to do.

Friends would also be sensitive to Louise and her needs. Apparently, though reared in the same home, she has been free to feel and express both negative and positive feelings about her parents. She has a fairly active group of friends her own age as a community where she can "let off steam" about her mother and dad. A mark of mental health is the ability to put into words the fear, hatred, and love one really has and to have someone to share them with. A real friend will spend time with Louise and listen as she shares the deep frustrations she must have in this situation.

The Scotts have apparently repressed most of their children's negative feelings, hindering their emotional growth. The short description of their family life suggests their attitudes to be mostly critical and sarcastic ridicule. This kind of parental attitude produces a climate very conducive to mental illness. Those interested in learning about a child's normal religious and emotional development and gaining insight into a proper parental role could read *On Becoming Children of God* by Wayne Oates. (See Resources.)

One of the finest ways to minister to mental illness is to become positively involved in the mental health movement in your community. A churchman could support his pastor's efforts to participate in its programs, and to attend seminars, conferences, and clinical training sessions. Through these experiences he will become more able to minister in depth to deeply disturbed people. He will become equipped to train his congregation, teachers, and leaders to be better ministers to children who are seeking friends along the pathway of their pilgrimage to mental and spiritual health.

Analysis by JAMES M. ROBINSON

Reverend Walters has established a good relationship with the Scott family. They have confidence in him and are willing to accept his advice. He can be of invaluable assistance to them in their troubled situation. The first contribution which he can make to the Scotts is to help them understand more about mental illness. They are greatly embarrassed over their daughter's need for psychiatric treatment. Such embarrassment stems from their feeling that there is a stigma attached to mental illness. If they can be led to see that there is no more reason for shame over mental illness than there is for physical illness, their embarrassment will be relieved. They would not feel ashamed if their daughter had to receive institutional care for a physical condition like tuberculosis. Neither should they feel embarrassed over the need for institutional care for psychosis.

The pastor can lead the Scotts to see that they must make a sincere effort to forget their own feelings and center their attention on helping Dorothy recover and maintain her health. Like so many others, they have become so concerned over what other people will think about them that they have forgotten that Dorothy must be their prime consideration. Some attention must be given to how Dorothy will be received when she returns home. If the family conveys a sense of shame to her and her mother and father are as harshly critical of her as they have been in the past, she will likely have need for institutional care again soon. Every effort must be made to build up her self-confidence and sense of personal worth.

Both Louise and Mr. Scott need some special attention. Louise needs reassurance that Dorothy's illness does not jeopardize her own chances for good mental health. Since being accepted by others is particularly important to teen-agers, she especially needs to have her embarrassment over her sister's illness dealt with effectively. Mr. Scott should be visited by a couple of men from his church to indicate their care and concern. A cash gift made up of an offering taken in his

Sunday School class and department would not only help out on the bills but would also be beneficial in leading him to see that Christians are not really hypocrites.

Dorothy herself needs the ministry of her church. When visitors are allowed her at the hospital, someone from her church should go by. Probably this should not be the pastor at first. Since Dorothy feels that her problem is more spiritual than mental, this feeling might be reinforced by a visit from her pastor. As her health returns, she will come to see that her trouble did not have a spiritual basis. Then she will welcome visits by her pastor and profit from them. During the latter stages of her recovery, his prayerful support will mean a great deal to her.

When Dorothy returns from the hospital, proper ministry on the part of her church is going to be crucial to her complete recovery. If she senses rejection by her fellow Christians, she will feel that God is rejecting her. She may even get the idea that he is punishing her for having been sick. To see where this will lead is not difficult. On the other hand, warm acceptance on the part of her fellow Christians will make her feel wanted and important.

That mental illness is so poorly understood is tragic. Why must it be discussed with muted voices and a feeling of embarrassment? Perhaps the greatest thing that Dorothy's church or any other church can do for those who are mentally ill is to help further understanding of mental illness so that the shame connected with it might be removed.

------•------

Analysis by JOHN ISHEE

From reading the case study, it is rather easy to pinpoint areas of concern which caused Dorothy's problem. Foremost is Dorothy's self-concept which was shaped by her parents and those around her. Dorothy sees herself as an evil person. While it is true that every individual has sin in his life, this does not mean that he is altogether evil. Neither does it mean that an individual should spend all of his time persecuting himself about how evil he is. The Bible is plain in its teachings about sin, but it is even more emphatic in its teachings about the worth and dignity of an individual. Christ died for our sins in order that we might have a proper concept about ourselves. Through him we can solve the problem of sin. The Bible says that we are to love God and our neighbor as ourself. Implied in this teaching is the idea that unless we have a proper self-love, we also have difficulty loving others and loving God. I see an inadequate self-concept as the heart of Dorothy's problem.

But analysis is one thing; prescribing a cure is another. Seeking specialized help for Dorothy is the wise thing to do. I am assuming that the hospital staff will know how to meet Dorothy's needs. My concern is with meeting the needs of the parents at this particular time and making preparation for Dorothy's return to normal life after she has spent her time in the hospital.

The parents need to have love and understanding at this point. Probably they will feel a sense of guilt over Dorothy's admission to the hospital. This is not altogether bad, because this sense of guilt can serve as a motivating force for them to change their relationship to Dorothy. Unless this relationship is changed, Dorothy may someday return to the mental hospital because she has been returned to the same environment that put her there in the first place. The parents need to be made aware of what they are doing to Dorothy's self-concept. Also, they need to be made aware of the fact that Dorothy has certain developmental tasks that need to be achieved at this point. I was concerned that nothing was said about Dorothy's relationship with her peer groups. Should not an eighteen-year-old girl be dating? Yet nothing was said about this. Should not an eighteen-year-old girl be given a certain degree of independence? While Dorothy grew, the parents failed to grow in their concepts of her. She needs to be treated like an adult, recognized as an individual who possesses inherent worth. She needs to be assisted in achieving the developmental tasks that face everyone at this age. Dorothy will probably need additional help at this point since she presumably has received so little help in days past. While Dorothy recuperates in the hospital, Christian friends should counsel with her parents to enable them to understand what they are doing to the personhood of their daughter.

"Why Me?"

James W. Hatley

In her neighborhood and at church she was known as "Aunt Kate." She had a proper name, of course, but "Aunt Kate" suited her better. Years before I became her pastor, her husband had been killed in a coal mining accident. Without children of her own, she had raised a boy left orphaned by one of the innumerable mine explosions, which was much the life pattern of those who made their living in the soft coal fields of West Kentucky. After Kirby was grown, a nephew was taken in, then Fred had died leaving the two alone. After Jim had finished high school and left for the army, there was another nephew, Keith, who came to live with Aunt Kate.

Aunt Kate's life had been filled with work. Cooking, washing, ironing, canning, making soap; one job coming immediately upon the heels of another, each one spilling over into the next one that had to be done. Now, at seventy-one years of age, she was alone. There was no one special to cook for, there was no reason to can food, and the house never seemed to get dirty. Aunt Kate had been free of any major disease and had been to a doctor only infrequently during her life. Of course, as was the custom in the community, she had sat up with friends during their illness and had visited fellow Sunday School class members while they were in the hospital. On one occasion she had nursed a brother until his death with cancer.

Her relationship to me as pastor was cordial. She never missed a service of the church and could always be seen in her regular pew. She knew that she belonged and did not require unnecessary attention from the church staff. She did not want to be "fussed over," she said. Aunt Kate had not taught in Sunday School and had no desire to be a "church leader." She was often asked to help with church suppers and youth banquets. She had a mild interest in missions and attended the women's organizations.

A knot appeared and Aunt Kate was troubled; she remembered talk she had heard from other women about cancer. The troublesome knot did not go away and after several restless nights and endless telephone conversations with friends, she reluctantly made an appointment with a local doctor.

The doctor did not ask, as much as he told, her that she was to check into the local hospital for surgery. As she spoke to me on the phone, she complained, in a light manner, about the doctor's insisting that she go in *this* Thursday. She then asked: "Do you think that means he thinks I'm so far gone he has to hurry up?" I assured her that the immediate attention was always the best and that it did not necessarily relate to how serious her condition was. We chatted for a few minutes. She talked about having to change her hair appointment and the need for someone to keep the class records while she was out of church. After the conversation, I remember summing up the experience as a conversation with a lonely woman, frightened and in need of reassurance as she faced a new and dreadful experience. I made a note to be at the hospital during the operation and called her Sunday School teacher to be sure she received adequate support from her friends.

I made a drop-in visit on Aunt Kate the next day. I remarked, as we were walking into the den, that I was on Hall Street and wanted to come by for a few minutes. We both knew that the visit was not that casual, but both of us seemed to want a low-keyed, slow approach to the real reason for the visit. After talking about the church, I said, "I'm free Thursday morning; would you like me to take you to the hospital?" She had already made arrangements with a class friend. I could tell by her expression that the offer had pleased her.

The subject of illness, hospitalization, and operations was now an open subject and ready for discussion. By her questions and comments, I discovered that she had some serious misinformation about hospital procedures. These rumors were causing considerable concern. She had heard that a person must pay in cash for his room when he entered the hospital, or that you had to sign over your insurance to them.

Aunt Kate had heard stories of the wrong person receiving a medication, resulting in the person's death. One of her friends had told her to take no medicine until she read her name on the card. She believed that she must hire a registered nurse or be left alone and unattended after the operation.

One fear after another was expressed and discussed. She accepted the facts given her and her relief was obvious to me. It was a good visit.

It was cancer, and the breast was removed. Aunt Kate received loving care and attention from a host of friends. She had flowers, cards, and visits. Members of her class brought her a robe to wear in her hospital room. On one hospital visit I called at a time other than visiting hours so I could be assured of some time of privacy with her.

She was excited with the attention given her and profoundly touched by each token of appreciation and concern.

She voiced the timeless remark of women her age, "You have no idea how many friends you've got until you are sick." Her interests were wide. She pumped me for local and church news. She inquired about several people by name. She asked me about a local election and my evaluation of an action the President of our nation had taken.

When the conversation turned, at last, to her and her condition, her reaction was that of denial. She had a strong need to deny any pain, any special need that the operation had caused. She was reluctant to discuss the problem of her illness as if by refusing to acknowledge it, it would somehow go away. "No, not me!" was the spirit behind her utterances. "I'll be using this left arm as soon as they take the bandages off, you just wait and see. I've seen some women give in to a few aches and pains but I don't aim to. They'll have to do a lot more cuttin' on me to keep me down in a bed."

I realized that I had not entered the room prepared for her abrupt outburst of denial of her condition. At first I thought that she did not know. She had not mentioned lab results and I did not inquire. I remarked on how well she looked and how well she had recovered from the shock of the operation. I did not join her in her grand statements of what she was going to be able to do in a few days. I felt sure that she knew the extent of her medical problems but was trying to make it go away through denial. I did not feel good about my visit. I had a sense of failure. I wondered if I should have been more direct with her. Should I have forced her to face the reality of her condition? Had I given her false hope by my silence? Was she asking me to help her in ways I didn't understand, in words I did not hear?

Aunt Kate was not ready to accept the reality of cancer. She could not admit to its presence; thus she hoped it could not control her. It would clear up somehow, some way. She wanted to keep her mind busy until she was up and about, and then everything would fall into its proper place.

Radium treatment made Aunt Kate ill, and the ordeal was a heavy burden to be endured. She did not respond to treatment and another hospital visit was necessary. On visits with her, I noticed that the get well cards were there again propped up on her nightstand, but they were fewer in number. Her class had responded again with loving care and a potted plant sat in the window. No longer did Aunt Kate reject or deny her illness. When we were alone and her words were spoken freely and in trust, they were words of anger. "Why me?" was a haunting question that she could not find a suitable answer to. Her concern was limited now to the local news. She was concerned only about the church and our revival. When the moments of prayer or Scripture came, the underlying question still was "Preacher, tell me—why did it have to be me?" She had lived a good life, she had worked hard, she had cared for others and had been faithful to her church. Then why did this happen to her? She mentioned a friend of hers, recently deceased, who had died suddenly and without obvious pain and with a tone of resentment wondered why she couldn't go like Ethel had gone.

I made no effort to control Aunt Kate's anger. I had no answer to the question, "Why me?" So I listened and wondered if I, too, would some day ask that question of someone else. Aunt Kate's anger was not toward God nor me, it was against an uncontrollable fate.

I remember seeing Aunt Kate back in church for the first time, much of the color of health vanished and her clothes revealing a great loss of weight. Rather than conserving her strength and coming to fewer church events, she seemed to be there every time the door was open, participating to the very limit of her endurance. With a genuine concern, I inquired if she felt up to this and she immediately countered with, "I'm here on earth to do the Lord's will; we all are."

I remember thinking that she was trying to buy a little time from God by going overboard on religious activities. The thought made me feel guilty for thinking it, but I knew that it was how I felt. I offered to drive her home from a church function, but Aunt Kate refused. Her reason was that she needed the fresh air. Any suggestion of help or any hint of concern over her health seemed to both anger and depress her.

Aunt Kate's field of interest had narrowed to her neighbors, to class members, and to a few select friends. Her vigorous church activity when put to voice sounded like a person that was bargaining with God. She was in a delayed pattern, one that sought to bargain, to stay the completion of her sentence of illness.

"I'm not going to bed again until I get the new class roll made out." And she didn't. "I'm not going to that hospital again until after our spring revival." And she didn't. "I'm not going to take any more x-rays until I visit the old Hopewell Church Homecoming." And she didn't.

The day came when Aunt Kate could bargain no longer for additional time. The pain was so acute that she was forced to seek relief. It was late afternoon when I entered her hospital room. The medication given earlier in the day had worn off and pain was slowly returning. No longer could she deny it, fight it with anger, or bargain for delay. It was there. She was no longer concerned with national or state events. She did not ask about the church or the news of the church. She was aware only of the nurses, the doctor, and whoever was standing at the moment by her bedside. Aunt Kate had entered a state of depression.

This forced state, the state of depression came suddenly and profoundly. She was weighing the price of death. She did not initiate conversations, nor did she assist in moving them along when someone else began one. Aunt Kate was concerned with the business of death. Slowly she was backing out of life, step by step.

Aunt Kate's depression affected me, even before I entered her hospital room. Before the visit I usually took time to select Scripture passages that I would use. I found that more and more I was selecting Scripture associated with death. I wondered as I drove toward the hospital: Should I speak directly of death? Should I pass on to her words of assurance that I had found in the Scripture? What should I be doing to help her? Do you accept her depression as valid and normal? Do you try to lift her out of depression in order to help the healing process? What would I want a person to do?

One day I noticed a difference in my visit with Aunt Kate. She spoke when I entered the room and began the conversation. She mentioned that she would like to see Kirby again. The *again* carried the sound of finality. Very little of her conversation was in the future tense. She did not cry and there seemed to be little or no depression. I started to remark that she seemed much better, but I caught myself and did not say it. Underneath, I felt that her renewed strength and interest was temporary.

If she felt pain she did not speak of it. Letters that had remained unopened during her state of depression were now opened. It was obvious that someone had read them to her. Visitors who had been ignored during her depression were noticed again. Aunt Kate made sure that several of the people that had visited her knew where her will was and the key to her front door. Several insignificant household objects that she wanted to go to special friends were mentioned time and again and who they should go to.

Aunt Kate made a pointed remark about how well she loved her navy blue dress, the one that she had bought for Easter, and she was saying in effect, this is the dress to bury me in. As her pastor, she let me know that she liked the 23rd Psalm and the "Old Rugged Cross." Of course, she didn't pointedly say, use this Scripture in your sermon and sing this song at my funeral, but the implication was given and received. She was, of course, withdrawing from life.

The final state of Aunt Kate's experience with illness and death was the state of total acceptance. I don't know when this state came upon her, but I noticed it immediately when I walked into the hospital room. Her simple words were, "I'm ready now." And she was. And she died.

Analysis by WALTER C. JACKSON

Every community knows the agony of fatal illness, and almost every family knows the devastating ravages of cancer. Aunt Kate's story is unique to her, but her situation is typical enough that suggestions for ministering to her can be generalized and applied to others in similar circumstances.

Aunt Kate's life has been marked by loneliness. She had filled her life with people and events which were quite meaningful, but as she nears the end of life, loneliness is a prominent part of her spiritual illness. Friends who wish to minister to her need should keep at least three principles in mind.

They should be genuine. If they visit her, they should *want* to spend time with her and not just go out of "duty." Very ill people are exceptionally sensitive to insincerity.

Secondly, her visitors should be regular. It is not necessary to stay great lengths of time, especially during the period of painful medical treatment. Frequent short visits would probably be the most helpful. Often, visits would not be necessary. A card or a personal note would be a better ministry. Finally, the visitor should be faithful. It is better not to promise at all than to make a promise and not fulfil it. As a person approaches the end of life and periods of doubt arise, your Christian faithfulness will be a testimony and reminder that God is faithful.

Friends who visit will do well to notice the pattern of Aunt Kate's illness. After receiving her bad news, she began a period of denial, not accepting the diagnosis of terminal illness. This is a standard pattern for all illnesses but is more acute when a dread disease is involved. She reacted unrealistically, almost grandiosely, believing that she would experience a miracle of healing. An alert friend will accept her need to react this way and assure her of his love and support even if the diagnosis is true.

The stage of anger, the "Why me?" stage, is one of the most difficult for Christians. Somehow we have gotten the mistaken notion that one does not become angry toward God. Remember, he created angry feelings along with the other feelings and pronounced them "good." When Aunt Kate's anger was expressed, it no longer remained like a pocket of acid within her, and God was still uninjured. A wise Christian friend recognizes this as a normal part of terminal illness, accepts the feeling openly, affirms that God understands it, and prays for her to move beyond it.

In the silence of her soul, Aunt Kate tried to bargain with God. "If you will do thus and so, I will do . . ." she reasoned; but slowly the truth was realized. Depression set in, and Kate walked through the valley of shadows. A wise friend would come more frequently at this time and occasionally say something like, "I feel like you are very depressed today, so I'm glad I came." The anger may return again and should be accepted the same way. And then, perhaps almost unheralded, your friend will have accepted her coming death as freely as Aunt Kate.

Again, a friend will be very faithful and may stay a bit longer as the patient's strength permits. The friend will be aware of the patient's need to be affirmed, her need to know that her life has not been wasted. She may want to reminisce, sort of write her autobiography in conversation to you. In this manner she will know that at least one other person besides God has seen her life as she sees it.

As the end approaches, the dying person may experience a deep grief. This may be due to leaving life, leaving a task unfinished, but it is closely related to leaving people for the last time. Those remaining behind lose only the dying person, she loses everyone. If, however, she has had a faithful friend like you, she will go to her reward with a deeper sense of peace.

———◆———

Analysis by JAMES M. ROBINSON

Aunt Kate made her way through the maze of chronic and terminal illness. She came to the place where she could say that she was now ready to die. The tragedy is that she had to

make so much of her difficult journey without any real help.
Her pastor had a sense of failure in attempting to meet her
needs. The boys she raised seem to have deserted her. She
needed a ministry that she did not receive.

Of course, it is too late now to minister to Aunt Kate. Her
church can provide a Christian burial and a ministry of com-
fort to her adopted sons, but this is about all. The question is,
how could her needs have been met more effectively during
the course of her illness.

Aunt Kate's pastor got off to a poor beginning with her. Her
phone call to him was not for the purpose of informing him
about the surgery. It was to seek support and assurance. She
certainly knew the seriousness of her condition. Everything
she had learned pointed to a malignancy. Yet, her pastor
never even discussed with her this possibility. He made no
effort to assure her of God's ability to sustain her and provide
for her needs if cancer were discovered. He chatted with Aunt
Kate about light, mundane things, when that was not what
she really wanted to discuss. When ministering to the chronically ill, an attitude of realism must be adopted. This can be
mixed with optimism, but it does little good to try to convince
the seriously ill person that he is going to be all right or that
everything is going to work out for him. He knows better. He
needs to be assured of the concern of his fellow Christians
and of God's constant care and sufficiency.

The pastor had a second opportunity to render an effective
ministry to Aunt Kate during the period when she was out-
wardly attempting to deny the seriousness of her surgery. He
discovered that she knew her actual condition and yet, once
again, allowed her to talk him out of dealing realistically with
her when she really wanted him to be honest. Even her denial

was a silent cry to her pastor for help. He could have said lovingly to her, "Now, Aunt Kate, I'm sure your doctor told you that your recovery is going to be slow and painful, but I want you to know that I will be seeing you regularly and praying for you daily." Those who are critically ill will often try to spare the feelings of others by making light of the consequences of their disease.

Aunt Kate was in dire need as she tried to grapple with the problem of evil. Her pastor felt that she was not angry with God but with an uncontrollable fate. Actually, to be a Christian there is no such thing as an uncontrollable fate. Every chronically ill person goes through a period when he wonders why God is allowing him to suffer. Aunt Kate's pastor could surely have helped her to see that God did not purposely and intentionally strike her down with illness. He could have encouraged her to rest herself in the assurance that God loved her and would care for her. He could have suggested to her that only God knows the ultimate answer to the problem of evil, but that faith in his love and wisdom is the immediate answer.

The terminally ill person deserves the privilege of being counselled by his pastor about death. Proper counseling will not increase depression but will rather relieve it. Once again, Aunt Kate failed to receive the help she needed.

Aunt Kate could have received help from her Christian friends and from her adopted sons. Every person needs some knowledge as to how to deal with chronic illness and then needs to use this knowledge as the occasion arises. However, in this case and in most cases of chronic and terminal illness, the pastor has to be the key person in the ministry. Surely, most will do a better job than did the pastor of Aunt Kate.

———————◆———————

Analysis by JOHN ISHEE

Helping a person face terminal illness is perhaps one of the most difficult things a Christian is called upon to do. The reality of death may cause him to so closely identify with the individual that he cannot remain objective enough to be of real help. I commend this Christian who tried to help Aunt Kate. I see principles that were followed which serve as a basis for advising church members on how to help individuals in these circumstances.

First, one must understand the process of grief. Generally, grief moves through several stages, the first of which is shock at the news of imminent death, or whatever circumstances produce the grief. Next comes denial of the reality of the grief. A person may simply continue to function as though the shock had not occurred. Next comes a period of "stabbing pains," in which the person's emotions may not be consistent from one hour to the next. Aunt Kate experienced fantasy, self-pity, and perhaps anger with God. This was followed by a period of depression. All of these emotions are simply a part of the process of facing grief. They are preludes to the acceptance of the grief itself. Aunt Kate moved through all of these processes in a rather logical manner. I commend the Christian minister for letting Aunt Kate be herself, rather than telling Aunt Kate about how she ought to feel and the type person she ought to be in this instance.

Second, in helping a person who is facing imminent death, it is not wise to give false hopes to the individual. When a person knows that death is imminent, to merely encourage the individual when there is no hope will destroy the Christian minister's integrity. Ultimately, the patient must face the reality of death.

Third, in addition to understanding the process of grief and avoiding the giving of false hopes, the individual who wishes to minister to a person facing imminent death can simply be available to perform whatever tasks he can perform. There is so little that can be done in a situation like this. The Christian can look for some practical tasks that need to be performed. What about Aunt Kate's home? Are there things that need to be done there? Are there other persons who need to be notified of Aunt Kate's illness? What other task can be performed that will give Aunt Kate some pleasure and a definite feeling that someone cares?

I recall Wayne Oates at Southern Baptist Seminary relating a story about a man whose Model T Ford was stuck in a mud hole. It seems that a man who owned a big black Cadillac came along and pushed the old Model T out of the mud hole. Then the man who owned the Model T spoke to the owner of the Cadillac in the following fashion. "Mister, I'm grateful to you for pushing my Model T out of the mud hole. And if your Cadillac ever gets stuck in a mud hole, I will put my Model T up against it and do my best to push it out. However, if my Model T is not strong enough to push your big Cadillac out of the mud hole, I'll get into your car and sit with you a spell just to keep you from being lonesome." There are some things that are beyond our ability to do. However, we can find tasks that are within our ability and perform them as best we can.

NORMAN L. BOWMAN is editor, Student Department, The Sunday School Board, Nashville, Tennessee.

RAY COOLEY is chaplain, Eastern Kentucky State Hospital, Lexington, Kentucky.

FRANK GRAYUM is editor, Church Training Department, The Sunday School Board, Nashville, Tennessee.

JAMES W. HATLEY is pastor, Second Baptist Church, Memphis, Tennessee.

REUBEN HERRING is editor, Church Training Department, The Sunday School Board, Nashville, Tennessee.

JOHN A. ISHEE is editor, Church Training Department, The Sunday School Board, Nashville, Tennessee.

WALTER L. JACKSON is Director of Chaplaincy Services, Kentucky Baptist Hospital, Louisville, Kentucky.

ALBERT L. MEIBURG is chaplain-supervisor, Crozer-Chester Medical Center, Chester, Pennsylvania.

JEAN POTTS is a free-lance writer who resides in New York City.

JAMES M. ROBINSON is pastor, Village Baptist Church, Oklahoma City, Oklahoma.

MICHAEL L. SPEER, director of stewardship promotion, Stewardship Commission, Nashville, Tennessee.

Complete Money Management Institute Booklet Library, available from Money Management Institute, Household Finance Corporation, Prudential Plaza, Chicago, Illinois 60601. Price, $3.00.

The Death of a Salesman, Arthur Miller (3v) $1.95.

How to Manage Your Money, R. J. Hastings (26b) $1.50.

On Becoming Children of God, Wayne E. Oates (8w) paper, $2.50.

The Organization Man, William H. Whyte, Jr. (13s) $5.95.

You Can't Go Home Again, Thomas Wolfe (9h) $7.50.

How to Fight the Drug Menace, Garman and Strickland (26b) $1.50.

The case studies in this book provide excellent resource material for group discussion in your church. The following suggestions are offered as guides for planning and conducting group discussions.

In any area of study, three general questions may be asked. These are:

1. *What do I know about this area?*—Each case study deals with a different aspect of ministry. Lead the members to share with each other the knowledge they have about these areas. This process will result in all group members receiving additional insight into the areas discussed.

2. *What is my attitude?*—How a person feels about another person affects the way he relates to him. Lead the members to be honest in expressing their feelings about the persons described in the case studies. When negative feelings are expressed, lead in a discussion of why the person may feel negative. This procedure may help the person to gain insight into himself and thus aid in overcoming the negative feelings.

3. *What skills do I possess?*—One of the primary purposes of a study of this nature should be to help persons to develop skills in ministering to persons in trouble. Skill development requires practice. Therefore, encourage the group members to "try out" new ideas as they encounter persons in trouble. You may wish to enlist members to role play the case studies before the group. Analyses of the situations may be conducted after the role play activities.

A record album, *When Trouble Comes,* provides additional resources material for cases one and eight. Secure this album and allow the group to listen to it before, during, or after the study of these cases. Additional suggestions about the use of the album are contained on the album jacket.

Date Due